MARRIAGE AND THE

BLENDED
FAMILY

RE-ESTABLISHING THE FAMILY UNIT GOD'S WAY

by

Dr. Alfred D. Harvey, Jr.

Marriage and the Blended Family

ISBN 0-9651783-3-1
Copyright © 2001 by
Dr. Alfred D. Harvey, Jr.
St. Louis Christian Center
870 Pershall Road
St. Louis, Missouri 63137

First Printing 2001
Second Printing 2004, revised

Published by:
Doers Publishing
P. O. Box 38700
St. Louis, Missouri 63138

To order more books, call
(866) 319-7460
or e-mail us at orders@slcc.org

DOERSPUBLISHING

Unless otherwise indicated, all scripture quotations are taken from the *King James Version* of the Holy Bible.

DEDICATION

This book is dedicated to my wife, Loretta, who has helped me be a better husband, and to my youngest son, Damon, who has helped me be a better father.

TABLE OF CONTENTS

INTRODUCTION

The message of *Marriage and the Blended Family* may not necessarily apply to all marriages, but it does apply to a large percentage of them. Teaching on divorce and remarriage is not usually done in most churches, and this may be one of the reasons so many Christians are having difficulties in their marriages today. Christians *do* divorce and remarry, even Christians with children.

The teaching outlined in this book is Bible-based and is geared to people who are saved, filled with the Holy Spirit, and attending a church where the uncompromising Word of God is being taught. But anyone who wants to improve their marital relationship can benefit from the information I share in this book.

The divorce courts are doing a land-office business, with no apparent relief. In fact, statistics tell us that one out of every two marriages will end in divorce. That means, that when a couple gets married, they have only a 50-50 chance of staying together. This is truly tragic, because many of these divorces involve children who are caught in the snare of their parents' mess-ups.

Marriage was created by God for the purpose of establishing the family on earth. The family is the backbone of any society, and the order or disorder of the family is an indication of the condition of a society. In other words, if the family order is healthy, then the society is healthy. Here in United States, the family as an important social unit has steadily declined.[1] Through the years, divorce has become more prevalent and even popular. Moral decay and the decline of the family are signs of the times in which we are living.

In my early years of ministry, I worked as a volunteer counselor and youth worker in the youth department of a large non-denominational Full-Gospel ministry. At the same time, I was employed as a police officer for the city of Los Angeles, where I had many occasions to deal with problem children. From my personal experience in dealing with these kids, I learned that the challenges facing our young people today usually begin in the homes, and often in blended-family homes.

There are various reasons for these problems, but I have noticed that when the children are unprepared for a new-parent situation, the problems become many and major.

Many years ago, I began counseling children who were having challenges in school and at home. I learned a lot from these kids, which helped me later when I began marriage and family counseling as a pastor.

Marriage and the Blended Family deals with couples who marry and one or both have children from previous marriages or alliances. It also includes information on how to deal with the "exes"—ex-husbands, ex-wives, ex-in-laws (and out-laws, as the case may be!).

[1] A heartening exception to this trend was reported in a recent newspaper article titled "Comeback for Two Words: I Do." The article noted that the flow away from two-parent families seems to have peaked and may even be heading in the opposite direction. In other words, the move away from marriage may have come to a halt. Interestingly, the article noted that the greatest change appeared to be in the African American community, often characterized by record low two-parent families. Jonathan Peterson, *Los Angeles Times*, The Nation section (June 12, 2001), A6.

Introduction

There is no doubt about it, a blended family can be a challenging relationship for everyone involved—that is, if the situations are not properly handled. But it can also be a great relationship if proper preparation, thought, and consideration are given before the marriage vows take place. There are a lot of things that should be in place before the "I do's" are said.

The primary purpose of this book is to inform those who are considering a blended-family relationship of some basic principles that will help them prepare themselves and the kids to be a successful family.

Most of those in blended families discover problems after they get into the relationship. But they could have alleviated some of their problems if they had acquired some understanding beforehand of what they were actually getting into and how to handle situations that arise and create problems for them.

Not too long ago, I taught a 10-week series on the blended family. The messages in this book are from that series. Some chapters may seem to repeat some of the information, but because I did not want to eliminate any of the material, I left it as I taught it. I have already received many reports of changed lives, changed marriages, and changed families from people who attended the original teaching sessions.

It is my desire that *Marriage and the Blended Family* be a blessing to every reader, and prove to be a survival guide for those couples with children who plan to enter a new marital relationship, and for those who are already a part of a blended family.

Dr. Alfred D. Harvey, Jr.
St. Louis Christian Center
St. Louis, Missouri

ONE

IMPORTANCE OF THE SPIRITUAL BACKGROUND

In a society in which divorce and remarriage is commonplace, a blended family is a most common occurrence. A blended family usually consists of a woman with one or more children from a previous marriage or a previous relationship and, of course, the male spouse. However, of late, it appears that men, too, are bringing children to these blended-family situations.

The dynamics involved in these relationships can be absolutely mind-boggling. It is sad to me that so little consideration is given to the children's emotional well-being before entering the marriage. Once the couple gets into the marriage relationship and goes about the tasks of daily living, it becomes very difficult to deal with what is going on in the hearts and minds of the children. That is why it is so important that the children be properly prepared to fit comfortably into the new relationship *before* the marriage takes place.

Young people can create havoc in a new marriage, not necessarily on purpose, but simply because of the emotional trauma they may be experiencing.

Normally, a child has a draw to the natural parent. Just because mom and dad got a divorce doesn't mean that the child is not drawn to the natural parent, even though that parent may be absent. When a new father or mother is introduced into the relationship between the child and the natural parents, without consideration being given to the child's feelings, the spouses may be opening a door for challenges that they had never anticipated. In other words, the children may not adjust to the new parent or the new family situation. The new spouses may be fine, but the next thing they know, the child is pitting the mother against the stepfather, or the father against the stepmother.

If there are multiple children involved, the problems can become gigantic. Added to that, the children may not get along with one another. All kinds of things can occur because no one spent the time preparing the children for the marriage before it took place.

I am not talking about the unsaved world; I am talking about Christian people. So I assume that the people wanting to apply the principles outlined in this book are born again and filled with the Holy Spirit. Whether or not the family members are Christians, the dynamics involved in a blended family are basically the same for believers and non-believers. But for the Christian, it is the application of the principles contained in the Word of God that can make the difference between success and failure. When you are going to put a child into a new family unit with a new father or mother, there are certain things that must be taken into consideration ahead of time if the family is to become a successful, functioning unit.

Take, for example, a relationship in which a man

marries a woman with a child. This child has a living natural father. It doesn't matter whether or not the child is seeing the father. The father may not even want to see the child, but the child still has on the inside of him or her the inclination to love that natural father. Now, all of a sudden, mommy marries a new man. He can be a good man and love the child, but that is not the issue. What has to be considered is what is going on in that child's mind.

In many cases, the children are not prepared for such a relationship. They are thrown into the new relationship and expected to respond in a positive way, which is often very difficult. A situation like that has a higher propensity for divorce than just two people getting married, simply because of the child factor and his or her lack of adjustment to the new parent.

It amazes me how Satan gets in and destroys a potentially good relationship because the natural mother believes the lies and deceits of the child and takes a stand against the new husband. This is a very common problem in blended-family relationships. The child lies about the stepfather, saying that he did something that he did not do. It is possible the child lied because he was not properly prepared for the marriage and did not understand what was going on, or the mother may have been in such a hurry to get married that she did not consider how the marriage would affect her child. You can imagine how problems are compounded when multiple children are involved. (For example, a woman may have a child from a first marriage and a child from a second marriage before entering a relationship with a new man.)

I call it the *blended family* because we are dealing with the coming together of different people and relationships within one new family. It may consist of a husband and wife and their respective families—perhaps the father, mother,

3

sisters, brothers, and relatives. Then there are the relatives of the ex-husband and, perhaps, the relatives of a second ex-husband, as well as relatives of the ex-wife or ex-wives. You can see how complicated things can become.

Before entering into a marriage relationship, both the spouses and the children need to be emotionally and spiritually prepared for a blended-family relationship. The spouses need to know what they are getting into. It is not that they cannot *do all things through Christ which strengtheneth* them **(Philippians 4:13)**; that is not the point. The point is, for the relationship to be successful, there needs to be a lot of preparation on the part of everyone involved before the marriage takes place. A lot of thought needs to be given to how the family will function as a blended family. It is no longer just two people getting married. In blended families, there are other people whose lives will be affected for better or worse because of the marriage. It has nothing to do with whether "I love you, and you love me." There are a lot of other things that have to be considered.

One of the first things I do in counseling sessions with couples who are experiencing problems with their children is talk with the parents without the child present in order to get some idea of what is going on in the family. Then I talk to the child alone, because most of the time the child will not reveal what he is thinking with the parents around. I also like to allow the Spirit of God in me to minister to the heart of that child. In most cases, I can get the child to tell me what he or she sees as the challenge. In the majority of cases, the challenge stems from the fact that no one ever considered the child's feelings from the beginning.

The child may say, "Mama came home and said, *'I'm getting married and you are going to have a new daddy.'*" Sometimes it is a shock and is very confusing to the child because he feels he already has a daddy and does not need or want

4

another one. Most parents don't give enough thought as to how this news will affect the child emotionally. It can be a very traumatic announcement to the child. This type of scenario can happen on either side of the mother-father spectrum, but in 90 percent of the cases, it is with the mother.

Imagine that a child (or children) loves his father, but for whatever reason has not had a relationship with him. Normally, in a case like this, the mother is not going to tell the child why she and the child are not with the father, so the child often feels it is his fault that the parents are not together and that he drove the wedge between mama and daddy. You would be surprised how often children internalize the split-up between parents and try to take responsibility for it. This split-up, if not explained in a way that a child can understand, can affect the child for the rest of his life.

The new spouses are happy; they go off on their honeymoon and do their thing. But afterward, when they get back home, they may have to deal with the child for years to come. The spouses need to be more knowledgeable about the problems that can occur in the marriage when children are involved. There are enough challenges when you have couples getting married without children. Just getting to know one another is enough by itself, but in the blended family, there are children and others with whom you have to deal.

Maybe you have gone through this; maybe you grew up with a stepmother or a stepfather and everything worked out okay. Each child handles things differently. Stepmothers and stepfathers are different. And maybe there won't be any major problems for you if you are considering remarriage. But in most cases, there are problems.

In this book, I want to cover some principles that hopefully will give you food for thought if you are anticipating remarriage and have children, or know of someone with whom you can share this information. There are some things he or she may want to consider before getting married. At the least, what I hope this book will do is help parents begin to discuss their marriage plans with their children and to do some things they had not previously considered doing.

Let us take a look at some scriptures that give support to what I will be covering in this book.

Amos 3:2-3

You only have I known of all the families of the earth: therefore I will punish you for all your iniquities.

Can two walk together, except they be agreed?

Matthew 12:25

And Jesus knew their thoughts, and said unto them,

Every kingdom divided against itself is brought to desolation; and every city or house divided against itself shall not stand.

Division and strife in a home come from within; they very seldom come from outside the home. Couples having in-law problems—mother-in-law or father-in-law —can never be challenged if the husband and wife are in agreement. That is why the Scriptures say, *Can two walk together, except they be agreed?* Not only does there first have to be an agreement to enter into the marriage relationship, but also an agreement to do it the right way, with the children being a priority.

My purpose in writing about the blended family is, first and foremost, to make people aware of the challenges that children face in new marriage situations, and of the fact that children can be the catalyst for dividing a family, which is just what the enemy wants. He will work through whomever he can to tear up the family. Satan does not like marriage, because God is behind marriage. What the enemy does is magnify divorce so that he can keep a man or woman with children single. Marriage and family are the strength and backbone of any society—however the family goes, so goes society.

God designed the institution of marriage in such a way that children would have both parents' influence. A father has things only he can impart into his daughter's life, just as he has things that only he can impart into his son's life. A mother has things she needs to impart into her son's life and into her daughter's life. God designed the "system" of marriage, if you will, for children to have both parents' input.

When parents get divorced, it is very traumatic for the children, especially in denominational church settings. In most cases, these churches talk about divorce so badly and treat divorced people as if they were second-class citizens, that the children of divorced parents sometimes feel insecure and confused as to the legitimacy of divorce. As a result, divorced people are sometimes made to think that they should not even think about getting married again, because that is a definite no-no as far as most denominations are concerned.

When the new blended family begins living together, Satan immediately comes in and begins to talk to the child. Usually while the child is lying in the bed at night, Satan tells him or her, *"He doesn't like you. The only reason he wanted to get married is because he likes your mama."*

Satan continues to talk to that child's mind and the child

starts feeling insecure and begins to do all kinds of things as a way to gain the parents' attention. So division comes from within; therefore, if a couple is going to have a successful blended family, there are some things that absolutely have to be in place. I cover these same principles with prospective mates in all my premarital counseling sessions. In fact, if the following principles are not in place, I, personally, will not marry the couple.

1. **Both parties MUST be born again.**

2. **Both parties MUST be filled with the Holy Spirit.**

3. **Both parties MUST believe basically the same things.**

Let me tell you why I believe these principles are so vitally important. You can be born again and filled with the Holy Spirit, but believe differently. For example, there is a denomination called Full Gospel Baptist. The members are born again, filled with the Holy Ghost, and speak with other tongues, but there are certain things they believe that other churches don't believe.

In the Church of God in Christ, there are born-again, Spirit-filled, tongue-talking believers. They, too, have their own doctrinal beliefs. In the Catholic Church, there are born-again, Spirit-filled, tongue-talking believers also with different doctrinal beliefs than other churches. In fact, all across denominational lines, you have people who are born again and filled with the Holy Ghost, but that is not enough. You still have to believe basically the same things. If not, you can have real problems if a husband and wife are not at least pretty close to being on the same page spiritually.

If they are not on the same page spiritually or don't have at least close to the same understanding of the Word of God, they may not be in agreement on certain subjects, such as tithing.

Tithing can be a big challenge for a family. For example, the husband does not believe in tithing and the wife does, but the husband has control of the family funds. I am sure you can see that this could cause a big problem in the family—what will the children believe? That is why it is so important that the spouses have the same understanding of the Word of God, including faith, divine healing, and other basic principles.

I am not saying that the man and the woman must be on the same level spiritually. What I am saying is that even though one may be further along spiritually than the other, they should still have a basic understanding that they are going in the same spiritual direction. That is vital. Women in my congregation have come to me saying, *"Pastor, I want to get married, and he is born again and filled with the Holy Ghost."* When I ask where he attends church, I often get the answer, *"Well, he goes to church over there at So-and-so's ministry."* If I don't know the church, I'll ask what they believe. I'll ask them to bring me a Statement of Faith or one of the pastor's tapes to let me know what they believe. You see, if a woman in my church is asking me, as her pastor, to marry them, then I need to know what her prospective mate believes. Why would I unite two people when I know they are not in agreement in what they believe? If I did, then I would be a party to their problems, if they occur later, and I am not going to do that. Therefore, I have to put forth some effort to find out what is going on with them spiritually, because most of the time, they are not thinking about these things. Somebody has to think about them. Marriage, done the right way, is great, and people should be happy in their marriages. But the enemy is busy tearing marriages apart, even among Spirit-filled Christians, and the blended family is one of his primary targets.

So, once again, the basic principles or requirements for two people considering marriage are: *They must be born again; they must be Spirit-filled; and they must believe the same things*. Both parties need to have basically the same spiritual background, and if they do not, they should not even consider getting married.

Now, let's say the couple is on the same page spiritually. There still are some other basic preparations that must be completed prior to marriage. You don't do these things after the marriage, because they will not work. Preparation is a key element to a successful blended family relationship.

---TWO---

THE PROPER PREPARATION

In the first chapter, I covered some basic spiritual principles necessary for the successful functioning of the blended family. In this chapter, I want to cover some basic common-sense principles I believe are essential for a couple planning to enter into a blended-family marriage. Please consider these issues very carefully.

1. **The person with the children MUST have a good relationship with the children before considering marriage.**

Let's say we have a woman with two teenaged boys who is at her wit's end about how to handle them. They are out of control. Then she meets a man, and he becomes her knight in shining armor. He is a good man; he is a born-again, Spirit-filled man who loves the Lord. They develop a relationship, and he decides that he wants to marry this woman, so he does all he can to get to know the kids. At the same time, she does not have a good relationship with her sons, so the relationship between the man and the boys is strained, but the couple gets married anyway.

Since the woman does not have a good relationship with her children, they can forget the boys having a good relationship with the man—all because she didn't do what was necessary beforehand. Since she knew she was having problems with her children, why would she throw her problems on this strange man?

Why? Because she is tired of struggling with her kids by herself. So she grabs hold of someone she feels can help her raise her boys.

I understand her desperation, but there are things she should do to develop a relationship with her children before bringing someone else into the situation. This woman needs to understand that if she has a good relationship with her children, she will enter into the marriage on a positive note. If there is not a good relationship with the kids, she is entering the marriage on a negative note.

2. **The parent with the children MUST be sure that the children understand clearly that the parent loves them.**

It is one thing to have a good relationship with the children, but that does not mean that the children know you love them. Let me clarify this statement. What a parent understands as love and what a child understands as love might be something totally different. If you want to find out if your children think you love them, just ask them, *"Do you think Mommy loves you?"* or, *"Do you think Daddy loves you?"* and see what they say. You might be shocked at your kids' response. You can have the best relationship with your children you think possible and ask them if they think Daddy loves them and they might say no. And then they will tell you why. They might say something such as, *"Because you did this, this, and this. I wanted a G.I. Joe, and you didn't buy me a G.I. Joe, but you bought my sister a Barbie doll."*

To the child, the fact that he didn't get a G.I. Joe equates to the parent not loving him. The child may not realize that the reason he didn't get the G.I. Joe was because he was being punished. He is not thinking about that. Something happened in his little mind to make him think that Daddy or Mommy does not love him, because they didn't buy him a particular toy, and he is carrying that thought on the inside of him.

To be assured of the parents' love is very important to children, especially children of divorced parents, because their "happy" homes have been destroyed. **The children absolutely must know that the parent loves them before the parent even considers bringing someone else into the relationship.** That means the parent has to work on it. He or she has to talk to the child and ask him or her questions. In other words, the parent needs to develop a warm, close relationship with his child before considering marrying anyone. This challenge is multiplied if there are other children involved. With multiple children, there are multiple personalities with which you have to deal.

3. **The person with the children MUST be absolutely sure that the prospective mate truly loves him or her.**

Let me tell you why I make this statement. People get married for all kinds of reasons, and love is not always at the top of the list. I don't want the women to feel that I am putting them down, but I have to be honest. As I said before, in many cases, women who have children will marry a man simply because she believes he is a good man and can help her with her children. That is not right. Why would anyone enter into a relationship under false pretenses and expect things to work out?

A man and a woman may agree to marry one another with the understanding that they love one another. However, if the woman is marrying the man for the purpose of getting help raising her children, she is actually entering this relationship under false pretenses. Love is vital when we are talking about any marriage, especially marriage and the blended family. The couple had better make sure they really love one another and that God is involved in the relationship. Actually, God should be the number-one factor. God ought to have brought the two together. If He has not, the couple can anticipate some major problems coming their way.

4. **The person with the children MUST be sure that the prospective mate loves children.**

The prospective mate must not simply love the children of the person he is marrying, but love children in general. Why would anyone with children marry someone who does not love children? I know of a situation in which a man had two children and married a woman who loved him tremendously but did not like children and did not want to have any children. She especially didn't like his children, but she married the man anyway because she genuinely loved him. Consequently, when you say, *"I love you,"* and everybody goes home together and everybody is in the house together —the man, the woman, and the kids—you can expect the challenges to begin.

When you are in a close environment, all kinds of things can happen. There were noises in the house that the woman had never heard before. The kids nearly drove her crazy. She could not stand to hear the kids running through the house, beating on the walls, and doing other things to which she was not accustomed. She just could not handle it, and so the couple divorced after a short time.

Now why would this woman marry a man with children, when she didn't like kids? That is not using wisdom. Those kids needed a mother, but she could not be there for them.

It is really easy to tell whether a prospective spouse likes children or not. Just watch his or her body language and their facial expressions. Watch how they act when they are around children. Watch how they talk to children, and when you two are alone and you bring up the subject of children, watch their response.

If you have children and are considering marrying a person who does not like children, that person should be scratched off your list. Otherwise, you are asking for big, big trouble.

5.   The person with the children MUST be absolutely sure that the prospective mate loves the children.

It makes no sense for a person to enter a marital relationship not knowing if the prospective mate loves the children or not. The prospective family has to spend some time together as a group. It is essential that they spend a lot of time together before marriage.

I'm talking about the right kind of time. Certainly, the couple does not want to do the wrong thing prior to marriage, either, because we reap what we sow. In other words, the couple should not start their marriage off on a negative step by having premarital sex. Yet they should plan to spend as much time as possible with each other as well as with everyone involved in the relationship so they all can get to know one another better. The children have to make a major adjustment prior to the marriage. The prospective family should do things together, such as go to movies, go on picnics, take walks, and go to restaurants, so they can see and experience one another in a variety of activities. There are things adults can do to develop a relationship with kids, such as taking them to church, to Sunday brunch, or just for a drive. The bottom line is that the person with the children *must* make sure that the person he or she is bringing into the family loves the children involved.

It is easy to say, *"I love you,"* but what about the kids? If the person doesn't love the kids, how can there be a good family relationship? There can't be.

Prior to marriage, consideration of the children must be first. However, once the parent in the relationship makes the determination that the marriage is of God, and that the prospective spouse loves him or her, and loves his or her children, there should be a shifting of priorities after the marriage takes place. After marriage, the husband's number-one priority becomes his wife; a wife's number-one priority becomes her husband—then the children.

There is a reason this shifting must take place immediately after marriage. If the couple does not go into the marriage with that attitude of shifting their priorities to one another, as soon as the stepparent says the wrong thing to the child, the first words out of the parent's mouth will be, *"Don't talk to my child like that."* And the thoughts of the stepparent will be, *"Oh, so now it is her [or his] child, instead of our child?"*

Let's say it is a man who is marrying a woman with a child. He is marrying the woman, but he is also taking on the responsibility for the child. He should have the mindset that says, *"This is my child also."*

If a woman marries a man with children, she should have the mindset, *"These are my children too."* Certainly she should treat them as her own natural children. And the man should treat the woman's children as his own natural children. But that doesn't always happen, does it?

"Those are my kids; don't you hit my kids." Now, all of a sudden, there is division in the household. *"What do you mean, don't hit my kids? We're married, they are our kids."* Most people don't have that kind of mindset; therefore their priorities become messed up.

6.   The children should be made comfortable with the relationship before marriage.

This is vital. In many cases, a man and a woman will develop a relationship that goes on for months. When they realize it is getting serious, or after the man decides he wants to marry the woman, then and only then do they bring the children into the relationship. That is too late. There should be no agreement of marriage before there is considerable interaction with the children. It is foolish to make marriage plans before this interaction takes place, but people do so because they consider the children second. It is not that the children should be first, but we have to understand that Satan will work through the children quicker than anyone else in the relationship.

Children today are smarter than many parents will ever know. In fact, if parents would sit down and really talk to their children (I always encourage parents to do this, but very few parents do it), turn off the television, turn off the radio, and just have a conversation with their children, they may be shocked at what their children have to say. The parent needs to talk to the children and tell them, *"I'm getting ready to marry So-and-so. What do you think about that?"*

I remember a counseling situation some years ago, in which this woman who had two teenaged daughters was going to marry. One of the daughters told her mother, *"Mama, he is a nice guy, but I don't like the way he looks at me."* Mama was foolish. She ignored her daughter and proceeded with the marriage. After a while, he made his "looks" a reality and raped the girl. The daughter had tried to tell her mother, but the mother would not listen.

That is one reason why children have to be made aware of what is going on, and they should be made to feel comfortable with the relationship. If they are going to be a part of the relationship, why shouldn't they have something to say about it? If it is of God, the children are going to be okay with it anyway. If it is not of God, we know that two cannot walk together if they're not in agreement, and a house divided cannot stand. If the relationship is divided beforehand, why would anyone want to make the relationship a permanent one?

It is amazing how many people will not make the children aware of their relationship; in fact, they won't even talk to them about it. Or they will tell the kids what is going to happen as if the kids do not have anything to say about it. For example, a mom will say, *"I am in love with Ralph, and I am going to marry him. And you don't have anything to say about it."*

Another thing about children: They sometimes can sense things the parent cannot sense, and the parent should not ignore their sensitivity. If the marriage is of God, it will be okay; if it is not, all the signs will be there. All the parent has to do is to give an honest look at the situation.

7. **If the parent is looking forward to marrying, then the children ought to be looking forward to the marriage also.**

The only way children can be made comfortable in the relationship is if the parent talks to them and lets them know in an open and honest way what is going on. Share with them decisions on important issues, such as where the family will live, and where the children will go to school if a change has to be made.

18

When most people get married, they do so with their own plan and purpose in mind—not God's. Most of the time, they are thinking about what they like and what they want to do. The woman thinks, *"He's tall, dark, and handsome; he has a good job; he can take good care of me."* While the man is thinking, *"She's pretty; I like the way she looks."* God has to be first. When the Bible says to **seek ye first the kingdom of God (Matthew 6:33)**, that means you have to seek God first in everything.

Proverbs 3:5-6 encourages Christians along this same line.

> **Trust in the Lord with all thine heart; and lean not unto thine own understanding.**
>
> **In all thy ways acknowledge him, and he shall direct thy paths.**

This does not mean to acknowledge Him in *some* of your ways, *but in all of them*. So you always have to seek God and get your directions from the Lord.

These are some things a couple entering a blended family should do prior to getting married. Most important is the proper preparation of the children for the new relationship and making sure that everyone is comfortable with the relationship before the marriage takes place.

THREE

COMMUNICATION PRIOR TO MARRIAGE

Communication prior to marriage in the blended family is vital. The following three areas of communication, I believe, are of special importance to blended-family relationships.

1. **What are the expectations of the spouses when it comes to disciplining the children?**

The parent should talk to the prospective mate about the disciplining of the children to get his or her view on discipline before the marriage takes place. Let's say the children belong to the woman. When it comes to disciplining her children, her input will be essential, because the children will naturally gravitate to her. She will have to get to the point where she can freely relinquish some of her responsibility of supervising the children, and they have to know she has given part of her responsibility to her new spouse.

She then has to determine how she expects her spouse

to respond in a discipline situation. Does she expect him to be the heavy, or does she want to be the heavy and he be the good guy? These things have to be talked about.

The woman, in most cases, has been raising the children by herself. Now, all of a sudden, here is a new person who is going to get involved in raising them. Now, can you see why it is important that the couple, at least, believe the same thing?

For example, what if one spouse does not believe in corporal punishment, and the other spouse believes the Bible? The Bible tells us outrightly to spank our children to properly train them. There are many people today, particularly those who have read psychology books, who say spanking a child is bad and criminal. They do not believe in physically disciplining children. If you do not spank children when they do wrong, the Bible says you hate them. (**Proverbs 13:24**).

The spouses should have certain expectations of each other based on discussions they've had and agreements they've reached before marriage. Normally, when a blended family begins to get together, the mother, for example, is going to have to "sell" her prospective mate to her children. It is not that there is anything wrong with the man, but the children, in most cases, still love their natural father, who may even visit them on a regular basis. Or he may take them home to spend the weekends with him and his new wife, where things probably are done differently than the way they are done at home with their mother. The children may have to learn two sets of house rules. You can see how confused things can get for these children. So there has to be some expectations as to how the new mate will relate to the children when it comes to disciplining them. These expectations have to be discussed prior to marriage.

The mother who is considering remarriage has to convince her children that she is making the right decision and that this is the right mate for her and the right stepfather for her children. Actually, it will be the prospective mate who will do the convincing by spending quality time with the children. When this is done, the children will be able to determine for themselves what type of father he will be. Don't think the children will not be looking and watching for what is wrong with him. They are looking for the flaws. That is just the way children are.

I remember when I married my ex-wife; her daughter, who is my eldest child, was four years old at the time. She actually convinced her mother that she should marry me. I spent a lot of time with her and we developed a real closeness; I would take her places with me because I love children, so it was easy for me. Her mother did not have to do much selling. Her mother was hesitant about getting married, but she agreed to marry me because her daughter was so in love with me.

My daughter didn't know her real father because he had never been a part of her life. Here she was, only four years old, and she was telling her mother how much she loved me. When we sat down and talked seriously about getting married, I said, *"Look, I know this is your child; I want to know how you want the child raised. We may not think alike."*

Right away she said, *"Well, you know I don't spank her very much."*

And I said, *"I know, but you need to. Are you telling me you expect me not to lay a hand on her when she does something wrong? When we get married and your child paints my car green, I am not supposed to do anything?"*

She smiled, but I understood her expectations of me, and I followed her rules, even though I thought differently. But at least we did get an understanding before we got married as to how she expected me to raise her daughter.

Most couples never talk about these things. Then they get married, the child acts up and the stepfather wants to discipline the child, but the mother gets upset and says, *"Don't you hit my child."* Then the man gets offended—all because they didn't talk about the expectations they had for one another beforehand when it came to raising the children.

Biblically, the expectations are clear and they don't change. Once a man and a woman marry, he is the father and she is the mother, and the Bible tells the father to **bring them [the children] up in the nurture and admonition of the Lord (Ephesians 6:4)**.

That doesn't mean the couple will follow what the Bible says. There has to be an understanding that when the mates come together in marriage, the children belong to both of them. They become "our children," even though the children may go off on the weekends with their natural father or mother. Can you see the challenges arising from such a situation? There are so many families involved in such situations. To make it work, not only do you have to be born again and Spirit-filled, but you had better be praying!

In many cases, the children may come back from a weekend with dad or weekend with mom, and will have to be retrained all over again in the house rules. This happens because they may not be doing the same thing at their father's house as they do over at their mother's house.

2. What are the expectations as it relates to the children?

I am not talking about the expectations of the children. I am talking about the expectations of who is going to do what and when for them?

Once my daughter was visiting with us for a couple of

weeks with our granddaughter, who is a very active child. My daughter likes to sleep late, and young children don't sleep late. At 7:00 a.m., they are hungry and they don't care what else is going on.

On the first morning after they arrived, my daughter slept in. I get up early. At around 7:00 a.m., I knew my granddaughter was probably up, so I went upstairs, knocked on the door, and as I expected, Kristi was wide awake. She had turned on the television and was just lying there watching a program. I said, *"Baby, do you want something to eat?"* Without hesitation, she was ready to go. So I took her downstairs and fed her breakfast. Later, I had to sit down and talk to my daughter. I said, *"Wait a minute now. You can stay here as long as you want, but we have to get an understanding about something. Your sleeping late and Kristi being hungry is not going to work."*

She said, *"Kristi can wait until I get up."*

I told her, *"Yes, I know she can, but she shouldn't have to wait. That is not the right way to raise your child. Your daughter should have breakfast—a good breakfast—not Pop Tarts or McDonald's."*

Now, my daughter has since learned better, so this is no longer an issue. I just wanted you to see that, concerning the care of children, the expectations of all parents must be clearly laid out and defined.

I know children who have been raised on McDonald's for breakfast because Mama did not take time to cook breakfast for them at home before going to work. So what are the expectations? Who will do what for the children? Will the wife or the husband cook breakfast for the family before going to work and getting the children off to school? Who will take the children to school and pick them up? Or take them to extra-curricular activities when they have to go? These things need to be discussed before marriage.

Everything should not be left for the natural parent to do, and the natural parent should let the prospective mate know he or she may have to help out in this area if everything is to function smoothly.

3. What are the children's expectations in the relationship?

You're going to have to talk to the children about this. What do the children expect? The children have expectations too. Maybe there is a boy in the family, and he might say, *"I expect my stepfather to play catch with me."* Children want to be taken places and have parents do things for them and with them. Children love to have parents spend time with them and show interest in what they are interested in. The problem in most families is that not enough quality time is spent with the children. Children have their expectations, and the prospective mates need to talk to them and find out what the children expect to get from the relationship.

FOUR

ROLE OF THE EX

Developing an understanding prior to marriage concerning the role of the ex-husband or the ex-wife is a very delicate issue. There can be a lot of challenges with ex-spouses, challenges that perhaps the couple intending to marry never imagined. One of the more unique situations I encountered is that of a man planning to get married who had not informed his ex-wife, who was living in the same city, of his plans. He and the ex-wife had a couple of children, who remained with their mother.

You may wonder what that has to do with the new marriage. It has everything in the world to do with it. Sometimes a woman will get emotionally "bent out of shape" when she feels her ex-husband has rejected her to marry someone else, especially if the ex-wife has no prospects of remarriage herself. If the man had talked to his ex about his marriage plans in the beginning, she might have adjusted to the new situation and accepted the fact that her ex-husband was no longer emotionally involved with her. However, this is not always the case, and one ex may not accept the idea that the other ex wants to marry someone else.

I know another man who had a great relationship with his ex-wife—that is, until he finally told her he was getting married. Things changed immediately. All of sudden, she stopped being nice to him and she stopped letting him see the children. She was very upset about his marriage, stating, *"He left me; now he has another woman. I am not going to let him see his kids anymore."*

With the emotional well-being of all the members of the blended family at stake, an ex needs to be prepared for the new marriage. Otherwise, there may be serious challenges encountered by the new family. In that particular incident, the man had such serious problems with his ex that he did not get married. In fact, the first thing his ex-wife did was take him to court to get more child support, stating, *"You may have left me, but you will not be able to afford somebody else when I finish with you."* These situations are very real and they happen all the time.

However, the fact that a man marries again does not mean it cuts off his responsibility to his children. He still has to pay child support; he still has to fulfill his visitation, and he still has to interact with his ex-wife. These are all a part of the blended family.

Successful Ways of Dealing With the Ex

The following are suggestions to help a couple preparing for marriage deal with the ex so that a harmonious relationship can exist between the couple and the ex:

1. **The person with the children has to develop an understanding with the new mate concerning the ex.**

The first thing a couple should do is talk about the previous marriage relationship and get an understanding concerning the ex. They need to talk openly and honestly with one another concerning this important issue.

Scenario #1 from the prospective male mate: "My ex and I have a good relationship. I see the kids on such-and-such a day; I pay child support; I am friends with her family. And now I am planning to remarry. How can I make my new wife feel comfortable with my relationship with my ex?"

In other words, the prospective mates have to make one another feel so secure and comfortable in their relationship that the ex will not be a threat. If the situation involving the ex is not handled properly, the ex can be a threat to the new wife or the new husband. My wife and I went through some things dealing with my ex. Everything was fine until I decided to remarry. Then my ex-wife's attitude changed, and my wife and I had to pray and work through that attitude. My new wife and I had an understanding, so together we dealt with my ex. If I had dealt with my ex alone, my wife would have been wondering, *"Why is he leaving me out?"*

All issues concerning the blended family have to be dealt with in an open and honest way so all the people involved are comfortable. The first thing the two people getting married must do is to get an understanding as to how they are going to handle the ex.

Scenario #2 from the prospective female mate: "I have an ex-husband and he has visitation rights once a week or once every two weeks. He pays child support. How much should I tell my fiancé about my ex?"

The woman and her prospective mate need to talk about these things. They need to talk about her relationship with her ex-husband in an open and honest way. Women usually do not want to talk about their ex-husbands, because most of the time, they have bruised feelings. They may just tell their prospective mates something like, *"I hate him; he is no good. He's undependable and I don't want anything to do with him."* But deep down, she may still be in love with her ex.

Even though she is getting ready to get married to someone else, an ex-wife still has and will have a relationship with her ex-husband as long as their child is living in her house. That is why it is called a *blended family*, and it can be a complicated situation.

The new husband also has to learn to deal with the ex-husband, who may have to come by often to pick up his child. Don't tell me these people do not need to get an understanding! They need to get the Holy Spirit involved if they want to have harmony and peace in the family. They need to bind the demons of strife and division, because a spirit of division can run amuck in such a situation. But Satan cannot get a foothold if the couple will prepare the way by talking things out together, and then together talking to the ex-spouse.

Scenario #3: There could be exes on both sides. If this is the case, imagine this, and it is not uncommon: The husband has children from a previous relationship and the wife has children from a previous relationship. The children have to leave the home of the parent and stepparent and visit one of the exes; the other children have to leave the home and go visit the other ex. When the children return home, the parents may have to work on them all over again to get them settled down into their family's routine.

Children can return home totally different than when they left. These are the things involved in a blended family and they have to be dealt with. So there absolutely has to be understanding and patience on all fronts.

It is not impossible to successfully deal with these issues. If you deal with them from a standpoint of communication, patience, understanding, and a whole lot of prayer, things can work out fine. Nevertheless, if you just ignore these issues and think that Satan is going to sit back and let you remain happily married with all these outside influences, I have news for you. He will drive a wedge between you and your mate so fast it will make your head swim, and you won't even realize what you got yourselves involved in.

Scenario #4: Let me complicate the blended-family relationship even more. Imagine that the wife has an ex-husband and the husband has an ex-wife, and they both have children from these previous marriages. Her ex-husband has to come to her house to visit his children, and her new husband has to go to his ex-wife's house and visit his children, but he stays too long. Everybody starts going berserk in the house. The wife starts wondering, *"Why is he staying over there so long?"*

This couple needs to get an understanding with regard to the relationships with the exes. That is why God intended people to be married only once. He knew exactly what He was talking about. People are the ones who mess things up. You can see how complicated things can become. You need to be sensitive to everyone involved.

31

2. The person with the children has to develop an understanding with the ex.

In the case of a woman with children remarrying, she should take the initiative in informing her ex of her plans. For example, she should tell him, *"I am getting married; his name is Ralph, and he works at such-and-such place. He really gets along well with the children, and I love him and he loves me and the children very much."*

No one can tell a couple what to do each step of the way or how to handle an ex, because each situation is different. Sometimes, however, I encourage the prospective mates to introduce the new spouse to the ex.

Someone might ask, *"Why should I do that?"* Remember, your children are involved, and you want to eliminate as many challenges as possible. In most cases, you can make the ex comfortable with the new relationship. It is when you avoid handling a situation that problems crop up. What has to happen is that the person with the children has to develop an understanding regarding both the ex and the new mate. That is paramount to a comfortable blended-family relationship.

3. The person with the children must develop an understanding with the children regarding the ex.

Children do not think like adults. They have a totally different mindset. Although adults do not think like children, if they would take the time to talk to the children for a length of time, they could find out how their children think. Children are loyal to their parents. The father can be a dog, so to speak, but the child still loves his or her dad, because children do not see things the way the other parent sees them. All this child knows is, *"This is my dad. Now, all of a sudden I have a new dad."*

The child's mind can go "tilt." He or she could be

32

thinking that the parents could eventually get back together. My son thought that for years, although I had married someone else. You do not always know what is going on in the mind of a child, so you will have to sit down and talk to that child to find out exactly what he is thinking concerning a new dad or a new mom.

Can you imagine the mental confusion that children in a blended family can experience? We are talking about little children, who cannot figure these things out in their heads. All they know is that, *"I love Dad, and I love Mom. I don't know why this is happening to us."*

Children become torn on the inside. They become confused and sometimes frightened when faced with a new family situation. In all this confusion, the two spouses come together thinking they are going to have one big happy family. But if the child's confusion is not dealt with beforehand, it will be hard for him or her to adjust to the new parent, and the child will express this confusion in special ways.

Let's say it is a girl, and she says to the father, *"I don't like your new wife."* In most instances, the man will respond, *"Oh, girl, you don't know what you are talking about. She's just fine."* In other words, the parent will ignore or disregard what is expressed by the child. In some situations, the child may have a legitimate complaint. In some instances, the wife will not act hostile toward the child when her husband is around. However, when he is not there, she will act differently toward the child.

It may be the same way with the man. As long as Mom is there, everything is fine, but if Mom has to go to the market, the stepfather may display an attitude toward the children that she will never see, or the children might display an attitude toward the stepfather that the mom will never see. Often, these things happen because the spouses and the children were not emotionally and spiritually prepared for a blended-family relationship from the beginning.

I want to emphasize once more that for a woman with children, it is vitally important that she develop an understanding with the prospective mate about her and her children's relationship with her ex.

She should express to the prospective spouse something, such as, *"I think it is very important that you [prospective mate] completely understand my relationship with my ex-husband and his relationship with the children. I love you, and my ex-husband is not a threat to our relationship. The children love their father, but you and I together can help the children understand that they are blessed to have two men that can help them grow up."*

This kind of honesty can get the marriage off on the right foot and the family off to a good start toward functioning as a complete family unit.

Let's look at another scenario. Let's say a woman plans to marry a man who has children, and she has children. He has his parents, and she has her parents. She has an ex-husband and his parents, and he has an ex-wife and her parents. In this grouping alone, there are several families involved. You can see why it is called a blended family. But it doesn't have to be a big deal as long as everything is handled up front between the two new spouses by talking about the situations that can arise with all these people involved.

The parent who is going into a new marriage absolutely must tell the ex about his or her new mate. This is where open lines of communication come in; this is where you stop all the mess. A woman, for example, should tell her ex-husband, *"I am getting married. There is going to be a new man in the house; there is going to be somebody else dealing with your child. It is no longer just you and me giving guidance and direction."*

I have seen situations in which the ex-husband was a good husband and a good father, but the wife decided she wanted a divorce for whatever reason. Then the ex-wife marries a jerk and gives him supervision over her children. You cannot tell me this does not cause problems! That is why people have to communicate all the way down the line. The lines of communication must go on and on until the children are grown and on their own.

Almost every situation in a blended-family relationship is unique, and every family is unique in some way. You have to develop lines of communication for your own particular situation, and this communication should be developed prior to marriage. You cannot wait until you get married to start communicating. It is too late then.

The woman with children has to do some smart talking when she explains to her child or children about the prospective mate. She is going to have to sit down and explain to her child, *"I know you love your dad, but now you are going to have a new dad too."* That may be confusing to the child. He may be already upset that he is not with his real dad, and now he is being "thrown" to some other man who is supposed to be his "new dad." Then the parent wonders why the child's grades suddenly drop in school and he starts getting into trouble. Basically, it is because the child really does not know how to handle these changes and emotions. No one has considered his feelings; no one ever talked to him about these issues, and no one ever gave him an opportunity to share what was in his heart regarding his parents' divorce and remarriage to other people.

I did everything I possibly could to explain my divorce to my son. His mother and I got divorced when he was two years old, and he was still asking questions about it when he was 12. Thank God, I had 10 years of being a good father to him. At 12 years old, he was at the point where he could understand and he never asked about it any more. He just accepted it. But we had to sit down and talk about the divorce and deal with it.

When a child is told that he is going to have a new daddy, he may think, *"Why? I don't need another daddy. I already have a daddy."* His mother should make every effort to make him understand the whys and wherefores of the new marriage situation. She has to make him understand before she gets married—that is, if she wants a peaceful and harmonious marriage.

To make the marriage one that will stand the test of time, the whole family has to be taught the Word of God. This is very important. As born-again, Spirit-filled believers, the couple should be in constant prayer for all the families involved. However, though they may be praying for these families, it does not mean that these families are attending a church where they are hearing the Word of God. It does not mean that these families are being taught the Word of God as it relates to these issues, and it does not mean they are being taught how to handle these issues. But as long as you do what is right, God will do the rest.

Proverbs 16:7

When a man's ways please the Lord, he maketh even his enemies to be at peace with him.

FIVE

IMPORTANCE OF BIBLICAL TEACHING

The Bible contains the answer to understanding and working out intricate blended-family relationships. Before I get into the marriage aspect of the blended family, let's look at some applicable scriptures.

Romans 12:2

And be not conformed to this world: but be ye transformed by the renewing of your mind, that ye may prove what is that good, and acceptable, and perfect, will of God.

Going into this relationship, the couple has to be determined to do things God's way and not man's way. The advice some marriage counselors and psychologists give people in blended-family situations can be confusing, misleading, and certainly not in line with the Word of God. In fact, their advice often causes confusion for all the parties involved. But if the couple will keep God's perspective before them, they will have a greater opportunity to have peace in the family, particularly if the spouses are endeavoring to walk in line with the Word of God.

Let's say, for example, you have a problem with your prospective mate, and you go to get advice from Grandma on your ex's side because you had a good relationship with her. That may sound comical, but people develop relationships throughout life, and they continue to value these relationships.

Here you are, ready to get married, and you are taking advice from your ex's grandmother. Do you think grandma is going to give you good advice? No, in most instances she will give you biased advice, because she loves her grandson or granddaughter, as the case may be, and may even be hoping the two of you might get back together. You have to be careful from whom you receive advice. It cannot be from just anyone. Both the spouses have to purpose in their hearts to do things God's way.

2 Timothy 3:15-16

And that from a child thou hast known the holy scriptures, which are able to make thee wise unto salvation through faith which is in Christ Jesus.

All scripture is given by inspiration of God, and is profitable for doctrine, for reproof, for correction, for instruction in righteousness.

Sometimes, instead of "for instruction in righteousness," I like to say it this way: "for instruction in living God's life the right way." That is what Christians need to learn how to do. We are talking about Christian marriages, and believers need to learn how to live the Christian lifestyle.

God never intended for people to get divorced, but He can turn a bad situation into a good situation if we will allow Him to, if we do things in accordance with His Word, and if we keep our priorities right. I believe this is where relationships become twisted. People do not keep their priorities right. They enter a marital relationship and forget what they are supposed to do.

For example, in a blended-family situation, the stepfather may come home and want to discipline the son for an infraction of the house rules. But when he attempts to discipline the stepson, the boy says to him, *"You are not my father; you can't tell me anything."* When the wife comes home she either has to side with the husband or the son. If she says, *"Well, he is my child and you don't have anything to say to him,"* the family is in for a roller-coaster ride, and the child may start acting up even more, because the spouses are not together. What should happen is that when the wife comes home, she should talk to her son and tell him, *"Look, he is your father right now. You are living in this house, and he is my husband, and you have to respect him. We are not taking your dad away from you, but your dad is not here. And while you are living in this house, you have to abide by the rules of this house, and you have to respect my husband."*

She has to do this in her husband's presence—not aside, but in his presence. The children have to see her stand in support of her husband. If the children know that the spouses are together no matter what, that divisiveness will eventually stop.

In this kind of situation, if a child is unhappy, he will usually act up when the mother is not around. That is when most of his bad actions come out. When the mother comes home and the stepfather tells her what the child has done, sometimes the mother will say, *"Oh, my child couldn't do that."*

I used to say the same thing about my son. I would say to my wife, *"Oh, my son wouldn't talk to you like that."* One day he didn't know I was home, and I heard him talking back to my wife, and that was the end of that. Still, I should have listened to my wife. To avoid situations like this, the whole family must be taught the Word of God as to their respective roles.

2 Peter 1:3

According as his divine power hath given unto us all things that pertain unto life and godliness, through the knowledge of him that hath called us to glory and virtue.

All things implies everything that is contained in the Word of God. In the Word, we can find whatever we need to know to have a successful marriage and a successful life.

SIX

AFTER "I DO," WHAT DO I DO?

Once everything has quieted down—the ceremony has taken place, the rice has been thrown, and the honeymoon is over—the family can then settle into the task of daily living. This is where all the preparation will prove beneficial, but there are still things that must be considered in order to maintain a peaceful, harmonious relationship where the family can grow together as one unit.

I believe the following points will help the family work toward this goal. There are three very important things that *must* take place once the couple is married in order to have a successful marriage.

1. **Both the husband and the wife MUST purpose in their hearts to live in one accord as much as possible.**

Genesis 11:1-4

And the whole earth was of one language, and of one speech.

And it came to pass, as they journeyed from the east, that they found a plain in the land of Shinar; and they dwelt there.

And they said one to another, Go to, let us make brick, and burn them throughly. And they had brick for stone, and slime had they for morter.

And they said, Go to, let us build us a city and a tower, whose top may reach unto heaven; and let us make us a name, lest we be scattered abroad upon the face of the whole earth.

These people were trying to build a tower that would reach into heaven. You and I both know that this is a physical impossibility. But look at what God says in Verses 5 and 6.

Genesis 11:5-6

And the Lord came down to see the city and the tower, which the children of men builded.

And the Lord said, Behold, the people is one, and they have all one language; and this they begin to do: and now nothing will be restrained from them, which they have imagined to do.

Although it appeared to be impossible for these people to build their tower, God said that if they were in one accord, they could do the impossible. Because of the unique dynamics involved in a blended-family relationship, it may seem impossible to have harmony in the home, but if the husband and the wife are in one accord, they can overcome any situation, no matter how bad things may appear to be.

It does not matter how badly the ex is acting. If the couple is in one accord, they can pray themselves into a better relationship with the ex. They can pray themselves into a better relationship with the child as well. They can have a happy family, but the husband and the wife *must* be in one accord.

When the child begins to act up because of a parental disagreement with the ex, the husband and wife have to take a stand together; if they do not, frustration and confusion will result on all sides. So when the child sees the husband and wife in one accord, there will be fewer problems in the home. There really is only one way a couple can truly be together. Each has to understand and be willing to apply the principles outlined in the Word of God to their marriage.

For a mom or dad who has remarried, it won't always be easy to keep up a united front with the new spouse. In the example of a mom and her son, yes, that boy is her natural son; she gave birth to him. The man is just her husband, not the boy's father. If conflicts appear on the surface, the mother will have a natural inclination to gravitate to her child and ignore her husband, and vice versa. That is why understanding priorities is so important.

Priorities say this: His wife is more important than his own natural daughter, and her husband is more important than her own natural son. When the children see they cannot break up this relationship, they will toe the line. But they have to see that they cannot break it up.

When my son was disrespecting my wife, I told him, *"This is your option: She is my wife, I love her and I am not leaving her. Son, I will sacrifice my relationship with you first. You can go to your mother's or do whatever you want to do, but I am not going to sacrifice my wife because you don't like her. It is she and I, and we are in it for the long haul. You are welcome in this house as long as you respect my wife."*

I let him know how I felt, and as soon as I let him know how things were, he changed. Couples experiencing a problem with the children because of their commitment to each other have to do the same thing. They have to live in such a way that the man puts his wife first and the wife puts her husband first, and the children have to know this so they cannot drive a wedge between them.

Unfortunately, that is not what always happens. Usually, the mother will gravitate to her child and the father will do likewise, so the children divide the family.

Do you want to know how to get God involved in your marriage? Walk in agreement—in one accord. Let me show you this in the Scriptures.

Matthew 18:19-20

Again I say unto you, That if two of you shall agree on earth as touching any thing that they shall ask, it shall be done for them of my Father which is in heaven.

For where two or three are gathered together in my name, there am I in the midst of them.

In other words, when the couple is in one accord, Jesus says, *"Hey, I'm involved, so I am going to cause this thing to work because the two of you are in one accord."* On the other hand, if the two are not in one accord, look out for problems! God cannot be in the middle of their marriage, so He cannot help them. He can only help when the husband and wife are in one accord.

2.   **The couple MUST understand the importance of prayer.**

In other words, the husband needs to be a praying man; the wife needs to be a praying woman. And they both need to work together to get the children praying also. Consistent individual and family prayer can do wonders in new blended-family situations.

Ephesians 6:10-12

Finally, my brethren, be strong in the Lord, and in the power of his might.

Put on the whole armour of God, that ye may be able to stand against the wiles of the devil.

For we wrestle not against flesh and blood, but against principalities, against powers, against the rulers of the darkness of this world, against spiritual wickedness in high places.

In these complicated relationships, there is a tendency for the partners to blame each other when problems arise. If it is not the couple's fault, then the spouses look at the ex, at the children, at the ex-family, or whomever. But the Bible says we wrestle not against flesh and blood, and the devil will work through whomever he can use to tear the family apart. People are not always the problem. That is why we have to remember the truth that we wrestle not against flesh and blood. It is the devil who is the instigator of many of the family's problems. We have to learn how to pray him out of our situations.

Just imagine you are in this delicate relationship, and you are not a person who prays regularly. **Ephesians 4:27** tells us not to give place to the devil. If you don't pray, what you are literally doing is opening the doors and the windows in all the rooms of your house, allowing the devil to come in with all his demons and set up camp right there in your home. You are allowing him to come in, because you are not doing the things necessary to keep him out, and the number one thing you have to do to keep the devil out is *pray*! It is amazing how many people are too lazy to pray and do not realize the importance of prayer.

Ephesians 6:13-18

Wherefore take unto you the whole armour of God, that ye may be able to withstand in the evil day, and having done all, to stand.

Stand therefore, having your loins girt about with truth, and having on the breastplate of righteousness;

And your feet shod with the preparation of the gospel of peace;

Above all, taking the shield of faith [we have to understand the principles of faith to be successful in life], *wherewith ye shall be able to quench all the fiery darts of the wicked.*

And take the helmet of salvation, and the sword of the Spirit, which is the word of God [and now you are ready for battle]:

Praying always with all prayer and supplication in the Spirit, and watching thereunto with all perseverance and supplication for all saints;

The Bible says, **praying always** (not sometimes, but always). So if you are going to deal with the enemy in your life, you are always going to have to pray. You have to take authority over the enemy all the time. You have to **submit yourselves therefore to God. Resist the devil, and he will flee** *from you* **(James 4:7)**. But you cannot resist the devil unless you first submit yourself to God, and to submit yourself to God is to submit yourself to His Word, and His Word says to pray always. That is how standing against the enemy for your family is accomplished. If you are not a person who has developed a habit of prayer, then you are going to have some challenges in your life, because prayer and the Word are weapons God has given us to deal with the forces of darkness. There are other things that will help—going to church regularly, being a consistent Christian, and praising and worshipping God. But scriptural prayer and the proper application of the Word of God are what really work.

If we want to stop the enemy in our lives, we have to pray and confess the Word over every situation. The more you pray, the more victories you will have in your life. What most people want to do when they come face to face with a challenge is to seek counseling from the pastor, so he can tell them they are not praying. When I ask those coming in for counseling how often they pray, I get answers such as, *"Well, I've been hitting and missing."* That is why they are in my office seeking counseling for their problems—because they have been "hitting and missing" instead of seeking the Holy Ghost through prayer as to how to handle their challenges.

We are not talking "Ph.D." stuff here! We are talking kindergarten stuff. This is basic. This is Bible 101. If you want to be successful in your Christian walk, you have to pray. If you plan to enter a relationship, or you are already in a relationship with all its complexities, and you are not a praying person, you are asking for trouble. There are so many reasons why it is so important to pray. Let me share just one statistic with you. There are more male-to-female child sexual violations in a stepparent situation than in a natural parent situation.

Take for example the situation in which a man marries a

woman who has a couple of daughters. If she is not a praying woman, she does not know what she is getting into. After they get married, the man might start thinking, *"She really isn't my daughter, and she sure is looking good,"* especially when daughters get to be around 15 or 16 years old. It happens all the time.

As a former Los Angeles policeman, I cannot begin to tell some of the things that I heard and saw involving incest. Usually what the stepfather would say when we made an arrest is, *"She's not my daughter; I didn't tell her to walk around the house in her underwear."*

Young girls often don't think about what they are doing or how they are exposing themselves. If they dress suggestively away from home, how do you think they are dressing at home? The mother needs to talk to her daughter and tell her, *"You don't dress like that around this man. In fact, you don't dress like that around your natural father. In fact, until you are married, you should not dress like that around any man."*

Girls have to be taught to be modest. They have to be taught how to be chaste, and it is up to the mother and the older women to teach them how to dress and how not to expose themselves. **Titus 2:3-5** states:

> **The aged women likewise, that they be in behaviour as becometh holiness, not false accusers, not given to much wine, teachers of good things;**
>
> **That they may teach the young women to be sober, to love their husbands, to love their children,**
>
> **To be discreet, chaste, keepers at home, good, obedient to their own husbands, that the word of God be not blasphemed.**

Many parents do not do this. They don't say anything to their children, and they allow them to dress any kind of way before anybody. *"Well, that is their father; he wouldn't...."* Friends, incest is on the rise; it is not on the decline. The Bible says things will wax worse and worse in the times in which we are living, but we don't think about these things until they happen. *"Oh, that couldn't happen to us; that couldn't happen to me."* It did and it has. Or it will if you do not act wisely and keep your guard up through prayer and the Word.

I know of another stepparent situation in which the unthinkable occurred. The mother loved her children, but she married a man who was involved in drugs. She didn't know it until after they were married. He was a drug addict, and addicts do strange things. He raped his stepdaughter, and because he didn't have any money to buy his drugs, he let the drug dealer rape his stepdaughter also. This is real life. These are Christians I'm talking about—not unsaved people.

I know of a situation involving a saved man who actually sold his daughter so he could get some drugs—literally sold her to a drug dealer—all because someone was not praying as they should have been. You have to understand that the devil wants to destroy us, and one of the most powerful weapons we have to use against him is prayer—but we have to use it.

3. You MUST always consider one another now that you are married.

Hebrews 10:24

And let us consider one another to provoke unto love and to good works.

Consideration is simply thoughtfulness — thinking about how the other person feels in a situation. The mother has to think about the husband and the children; the father has to think about the wife and the children. In a blended-family situation, everyone has to think about everyone else. The parents have to realize that this is a different situation. These children are thrown into this relationship, and they will need help in adjusting to it.

You cannot go into this type of relationship with a selfish attitude. You *must* be aware of the other person's feelings. **Philippians 2:3** tells us that we are to "esteem" others as better than ourselves. In other words, we should give others first preference. But how often do we really do that? What most of us do is think about ourselves first. *"I'm important, and I don't like the way he talked to me."* You could have been wrong; did you ever think about that? Still that is never the issue. The issue is what we don't like. We get angry with the children, but we don't consider what they may be going through.

When you throw children into a traumatic situation such as a blended family, it may change their behavior. They may begin to act differently. The first thing some parents want to do is to just spank the children when they act up. What the parents need to do is recognize that the children may be going through something and need tender loving care and kind words to help them get over the hump during this adjustment period. Most parents just react, and in their reacting, they make the situation worse.

Haggai 1:5-7

Now therefore thus saith the Lord of hosts; Consider your ways.

Ye have sown much, and bring in little; ye eat, but ye have not enough; ye drink, but ye are not filled with drink; ye clothe you, but there is none warm; and he that earneth wages earneth wages

to put it into a bag with holes.

Thus saith the Lord of hosts; Consider your ways.

If you are not producing positive results based upon what you are sowing, something is wrong somewhere, and you need to consider your ways. If you are in a relationship where there is chaos—the children are acting up, the wife or the husband is acting up—something is wrong somewhere, and the couple needs to take stock and examine the whole family situation. We know the devil is behind much of the confusion, but it could also be you. (You might want to blame some of what is wrong on that "devil" in the mirror!)

There can be a change in the spouse's behavior toward one another as well, especially if the wife does not like some of the things her new husband is doing or vice versa. The lack of harmony between the spouses can affect the children's actions.

I'm reminded of a situation in which the wife did not like something her husband was doing. She made the cardinal mistake of telling her ex-husband about it. That is a no-no. You keep your mess in your house; you don't tell your mama, sister, brother, or *anybody*.

There is a good message in this. People talk too much; women talk too much to their mothers about their husbands. Your mother should not know anything that is going on in your house. If she does, you are wrong, because she is hearing only one side—your side—and it could be tainted. What happens many times in these tattletale situations is that the mother-in-law ends up hating the son-in-law, when, actually, it could very well be her daughter who is in the wrong. That is not right.

Unless there is a situation of physical abuse, child molestation, or some other such life-threatening situation, all the business concerning the family should be kept inside the home. Many women just have to get on the telephone and talk to somebody. I know I'm probably stepping on some toes, so to speak, but I am just telling the truth: there's the telephone, telegraph, and tell-a-woman! The only thing she is doing is causing her and her family more problems. I have heard all of the excuses.

"Well, I have to talk to someone."

That's why you got married — talk to your mate!

"He will not listen."

Yes he will. Your problem is that you have not learned how to talk to him the right way. You have been nagging him so much that he stopped listening to you. You have to talk to him so he will listen. I'll bet you know how to talk to him when you want something. I'll bet you know how to ask for a new dress or a new car. So why can't you deal with the other issues of life in the same easy manner? If you absolutely must get help, go to your pastor, who will keep what you say confidential.

It always amazes me how people run into situations in the family but they take it outside the family and expect the situation to be resolved. It is not going to be resolved outside the family. If you need a mediator, see your pastor.

No one wants to be told they are wrong, but if I feel the wife is wrong, I will tell her so; if I feel the husband is wrong, I will tell him so. Most of the time, when a couple has a counseling session with the pastor, they both want to be told they are right. If everyone were doing everything right, there would not be a need for counseling.

In fact, from now on, when a couple walks into my office, the first statement that will come out of my mouth will be, *"Both of you are doing something wrong. So let's just understand that from the beginning. Let's just figure out what you, the wife, are doing wrong, and what you, the husband, are doing wrong, and let's just try to correct it, because both of you are doing something wrong."*

Since both can be wrong, when one or the other picks up the telephone and calls Mama, it only makes a bad situation worse because Mama will call someone too. Mama will call the sister, and the sister will call her girlfriend, and pretty soon the family's business is all over town. People on your job know exactly what is going on in your bedroom because you told Mama.

Then some women will call other women and say, *"Whatever you do, don't tell anybody."* The other party may even make a promise not to tell, saying, *"I won't tell a soul."* I'll guarantee you that as soon as she hangs up the phone, she will be calling someone else and telling her what is going on. To say, *"Don't tell,"* is like telling her to tell! Don't do that! Keep your business in your home.

Men don't need to talk to anybody else, either. The reason I say "consider your ways" is, there are so many things that come into play in these situations to which thought has to be carefully given or the situation could spiral out of control and the damage be irreparable.

The husband does not need to have female (or male) friends with whom he has to talk, and the wife does not need to have male (or female) friends with whom she has to talk. If there is a need to talk to others, the husband and wife need to talk to each other. To have friends with whom you share things about your marriage is a mistake, and you are violating the sanctity of your marital relationship. Watch it! You may tell your friend so much that the next thing you know, she may be sleeping with your husband. Believe me, it happens more than people think. She may get to know your husband far too well. Why? Because you told her all about him. While you were telling her all these things, the devil got into the conversation, and the friend was sitting on the other end of the phone, thinking, *"That's not so bad to me. That sounds pretty good to me. That would be okay with me, because my ex-husband would do this, that, and the other."* All these things were going around in her head, and while you were fussing, she was thinking, *"He sounds like a pretty good man to me."*

If spouses would talk less to others and more to each other, they would solve a lot of problems. Keep your business in your home.

These are things that can tear up anybody's family. As soon as there is a disagreement or a challenge in the marriage, most spouses look for someone to talk to, rather than talking to each other. They should be saying to each other, *"We have a problem; let's talk to one another."* Instead, the couple gets angry with each other, then ends up talking to someone else about the problem. That does not help the relationship because the spouses are only telling things from their point of view, and there are always two sides to every story. I like to say it this way, *"There is his version, there is her version, and then there is the correct version."* The correct version is somewhere between his version and her version. She cannot tell her version without thinking about herself, and he cannot tell his version without thinking about himself, so the truth is somewhere in the middle.

The solution to any situation lies in the spouses being able to come together, listen to one another attentively, consider one another, and be willing to arrive at an amicable resolution.

SEVEN

RESPONSIBILITIES OF THE FATHER

his is a statement I feel is essential for Christian
men to understand: *Every Christian man should be
an example or role model for his children to follow.* Children
should not have to look outside the family for role models.
The role models should be the father and the mother, and
these role models should be in every Christian home.

It is high time that we have role models within the
Christian family and within the Church instead of having
some public, celebrity or athletic figure as a role model. Why
can't born-again, Spirit-filled fathers and mothers in the home
be godly examples? Well, they will be when they learn how
to apply the Word of God to their lives and to bring their
children up the right way.

I grew up under the rule, *"Do as I say, and not as I do."*
I don't say this is necessarily a bad rule, but I often saw
some of my relatives doing things that should not be done

in front of children. For example, when I was about eight or nine years old, I saw family members drinking beer and champagne during the Christmas holidays, and I wanted some. That is not setting a good example. Children should not see their parents or relatives drinking or smoking, because it gives the idea that it is okay to do these things, and children will follow that example. Drinking and smoking are dangerous to a person's health, so we don't want to foster that kind of thinking among our young people. Christians have to remember that their bodies are the temples of the Holy Ghost, and God dwells in them (**1 Corinthians 6:19**).

In a blended-family situation, it is even more important that the man be an example to his wife and children. The reason it is more important is the children have already gone through one, possibly even two or more, situations in which the family has been ripped apart. They have seen their parents go through a divorce. A child goes through a very traumatic time when parents get divorced. The parents also need to understand that children going through a divorce often carry their confusion and emotional pain into their adult lives.

As I said before, God never intended for couples to divorce. God knows what happens when there is a tearing apart. The Scriptures say that when two people get married, they become one. In **Ephesians 5:31**, the word *joined* literally means, "to stick together like glue." Imagine taking two pieces of paper and gluing them together. It is very difficult to pull the papers apart. That is why divorce is so painful, because there is an emotional tearing. Why? Because two people became one and now they are being torn apart, and that is not a pleasant thing. More importantly, we cannot really begin to understand how a child feels when the parents separate. However, I know how it feels, because I went through it.

My father died when I was nine years old. My mother remarried, and I later experienced the ripping apart of divorce. It was not a fun thing, to say the least. I was older at that time, but to see my mother go through that was very painful to me. I saw how my stepfather treated her when they separated, and I didn't like him for that. Children go through all kinds of emotions when a divorce occurs. You may not see them act differently, because children will not always verbalize their feelings, but the emotions are there.

It is very important that when you choose a new mate that the two of you live circumspectly before the children. The new parent must be an example for the children to follow because, in most instances, the natural father will not be there.

For illustrative purposes, let's use a divorced woman with a child. She is preparing to remarry, and her prospective mate could be a wonderful man, but that has nothing to do with it. Let's say the child really loves his natural father, but this new man is in the relationship. Simply because of the relationship, all kinds of confusing things will be going through the mind of the child, depending on his age. They love their real father, but they think, *"We are in this new house, and Mom is in the bed with this strange man, and Daddy is someplace else."*

Again, this shows why parents have to prepare children for the relationship. It can be frightening for them. Even with preparation, the child at first will feel strange when the new father moves into the home, or the mother and child move into the new parent's home.

Hopefully, the mother will have a special enough relationship with the child that he will talk about his feelings with regard to the new relationship. If not, the child can be adversely affected.

I encourage the man who is going into a blended-family marriage to purpose in his heart to be an example

57

for the children to follow. He has to be a role model, a godly man, and he has to be a loving man. He has to try to do for that child what, perhaps, the child's real father did not do for him or her. The real father may have left the mother or had a mutual parting, so the new spouse has to replace, in the mind of that child, some security and stability. That is a full-time job. The father should be the one who talks to the child about life. Most parents do not talk to their children about life; they let the television and the streets teach them.

Remember the term, *"the birds and the bees?"* I wonder how many of us have actually had our fathers and mothers sit down and explain to us about the birds and the bees? No one ever explained them to me. I heard the phrase, *"the birds and the bees,"* but I really didn't know what it meant.

One day in the sixth grade, I was on the playground, and I saw the other kids pointing up toward the roof of the school. I looked up and I saw two pigeons mating, and I thought, *"That is probably what people mean about the birds and the bees."* That was the terminology used for sex when I was growing up. However, no one ever talked to me about anything, and that is usually the case in most families. We, as parents, have the responsibility to teach our children about all aspects of life.

One thing parents should teach their kids is how they should carry themselves—how to smile, how to look, how to act, how to walk, and how to talk. Many parents don't even talk to their kids about their attitude, and attitude is what gets people in trouble. They just let their kids look and act any kind of way. That is one thing I will say for my parents: We were not allowed to have a bad attitude. We were expected to have smiles on our faces, and we always had to look at our parents with respect. There was none of this rolling your eyes or sucking your teeth or anything like that. In fact, if they even thought we were going to do that, you could see the hairs on their arms rise up: *"Boy, have you lost your mind?"*

We were not allowed to act disrespectful to them or any adult in authority in any way. Today, children do it all the time, and parents just ignore their actions. Children have to be taught how to act, and it is a full-time job.

I am finding that men are not teaching their sons about personal hygiene, such as taking a shower every day, putting on deodorant, wearing cologne, brushing their teeth, washing their face, and combing their hair. These are just basic, everyday things that our children must learn to do. Parents need to teach their children about personal hygiene and how to take care of themselves.

There are a lot of things girls need to be taught. I believe you have to spend more time teaching girls than boys. Mothers need to teach their daughters how to dress for church. Some women wear all kinds of skimpy clothes to Sunday or midweek services. It amazes me how some women never think about the clothes they are wearing that allow their undergarments to show through—either the lines from their underpants, their bra straps, or they will wear a sheer blouse and not have on the appropriate undergarment.

We have to teach our young people how to be godly. They do not learn how to be godly simply by osmosis; they have to be taught. In the **Book of Titus** (I will cover this in more detail in Chapter 8, Responsibilities of the Mother), it says women have to be taught how to love their husbands, to be keepers at home, how to be discreet and chaste. They have to be taught to be modest; they just don't learn these things by themselves.

Your daughters will not learn this on the streets or from their girlfriends. They have to learn these things at home from their parents. People don't just acquire high class. High class is acquired through teaching and through discipline.

It is easy to look at a person and see one who has class and one who doesn't. Women without class do not care how they sit or how they carry themselves.

Stop and think about yourself. Many of the things you did not learn at home hurt you later in life. Some kids cannot get a job, because no one taught them how to dress when going to look for a job. No one taught them how to present themselves in an interview; no one taught them how to speak clearly. Slang and Ebonics are not going to get you a job. Employers want people who can represent their company in a positive way. Employers are always looking for special people. Parents have the responsibility to teach their children to be special. Parents have the responsibility to teach their children and to prepare them for life.

Deuteronomy 3:28

But charge Joshua, and encourage him, and strengthen him: for he shall go over before this people, and he shall cause them to inherit the land which thou shalt see.

Both the father and mother have the responsibility to encourage their children. Encouragement is simply positive motivation that causes a child to act in a positive way. Everyone needs encouragement at one time or another, especially our children. We tell our children to do a lot of things, but how often do we encourage them?

When I was growing up, I don't ever remember hearing a word of encouragement from anyone. I was told to do a lot of things, I was told I had better do them, and certain things happened when I didn't do as I was told. But I don't know if I ever heard any words of encouragement.

Discipline without encouragement is a waste of time. You have to do both. We can be fathers, and we can be mothers, and we can tell our children what to do, but when was the last time we encouraged our children to help build in them some self-respect to the point where they thought they were special?

I can tell you why you don't encourage your children enough; probably because you were not encouraged enough when you were growing up. Faith comes by hearing, so if you did not hear any encouragement, how are you going to provide encouragement for someone else? The only reason I learned to encourage my children is, I went to a church that taught this principle, and I learned how to put it into practice in my own life.

We have to encourage our children. Our children will make mistake after mistake, and they are going to fall on their faces, because this is all part of living. But it is how we, as parents, respond to their mistakes that will affect them positively or negatively. You can encourage your child even after he makes a mistake, or you can tear him down.

I was thinking about this one day: I am an employer, and we have a number of employees at the church. I try to be the kind of employer who encourages my employees and tells them they are doing a good job. Yes, employees like being patted on the back, but they also like being patted in their pocketbooks. Let's be honest: You can tell me I'm doing a good job, but when it comes time for a raise, *show* me I'm doing a good job.

If employees are doing a good job, they expect to be compensated. And if they are doing a good job, they should be compensated. God compensates us when we do a good job. Encouragement motivates people to continue to do well. Many parents have tried to motivate their children by threatening them. That does not go very far. They may get the job done, but they won't do it with joy. Encouragement causes children to work even harder, because they want to please their parents. They do not do it out of fear of the parents; they want to make their parents happy. Why? Because their parents patted them on the back.

When parents encourage their children, it shows the children that the parents care about them and love them, and that they have an interest in what they are doing. If the only thing the children ever hear from the parents is, *"Do this, do that,"* and *"I'm going to get you if you don't do this or that,"* and they never hear any words of encouragement, they will develop sullen and bad attitudes.

For example, when a child cleans up his room, he hears, *"Well, you should have been doing that all the time."* It seems as if it takes children forever to learn how to clean the kitchen properly, but when they finally do a good job, they hear, *"It's about time."* That is not encouragement. Our young people need encouragement.

When I was growing up, my stepfather gave me a rough time, but I turned the situation into a positive one for myself. I turned it into a positive one because I wanted to achieve in spite of him. I developed a hate; it was an, *"I'm going to show you,"* kind of hate. It motivated me to be a high achiever in everything I set my mind to do. Many children take the attitude, *"Fine, I can't make you happy; I'm not doing anything,"* and they sit around doing nothing. Then they blame the parents for their failure in life—all because parents have not learned how to offer encouragement and support to the child.

I'll tell you something else, husbands and wives need encouragement. Everyone likes a pat on the back, *"You are doing a good job; I really appreciate you." "Baby, that was a good meal—that was really good."* This is what a wife appreciates hearing from her husband instead of simply leaving the table without a word and heading to the den to prop his feet up in front of the television, not showing even enough concern to help clean up the dinner dishes. In the Body of Christ, we need to be more encouraging to one another, but especially to our children.

Many children come into the blended-family relationship hurting. The parents may not be aware of it, but they are, and encouragement can help pull them out of their hurt. A little pat on the back, a little show of affection to let them know, *"I care about you,"* can do wonders.

When the child says, *"Dad, I got straight A's,"* the father ought to rant and rave, *"Boy, you got straight A's! Let's celebrate; let's go out to dinner. Where do you want to go eat?"* This is the kind of encouragement children need. It will motivate them to work even harder the next time. I guarantee that if you will begin to encourage your children, you will see a change in them that will surprise you. They are looking for someone to appreciate them. Encouragement, like love, should begin with the parents in the home.

Remember, fathers: Be there for your children. They need you. They need your influence. They need your guidance. They need your wisdom. They need your support. And most of all, they need your expressions of love towards them. In the blended-family scenario, they need to see you loving their mother. This is also very important. It will add tremendous stability to their lives. Simply be the man of God our Heavenly Father desires you to be, and everything will work out fine.

EIGHT

RESPONSIBILITIES OF THE MOTHER

Ephesians 5:25-33:

Husbands, love your wives, even as Christ also loved the church, and gave himself for it;

That he might sanctify and cleanse it with the washing of water by the word,

That he might present it to himself a glorious church, not having spot, or wrinkle, or any such thing; but that it should be holy and without blemish.

So ought men to love their wives as their own bodies. He that loveth his wife loveth himself.

For no man ever yet hated his own flesh; but nourisheth and cherisheth it, even as the Lord the church:

For we are members of his body, of his flesh, and of his bones.

For this cause shall a man leave his father and mother, and shall be joined [or "stick to like glue"] *unto his wife, and they two shall be one flesh.*

This is a great mystery: but I speak concerning Christ and the church.

Nevertheless let every one of you in particular so love his wife even as himself; and the wife see that she reverence her husband.

These verses are a powerful statement to men, but there is a statement here to the women that needs to be preached from the top of the roof: *And the wife see that she reverence her husband.*

Let's look at an example of *reverence* in the Bible:

1 Peter 3:1

Likewise, ye wives, be in subjection to your own husbands; that, if any obey not the word, they also may without the word be won by the conversation of the wives.

This is one scripture that most women find hard to follow. And the reason they find it difficult to do is, they may not like how their husbands are treating them. This is why following the Word of God is so vitally important for the whole family. God does not tell us to do something based on what the other person is doing. God tells husbands **to love your wives even as Christ also loved the church.** Even if a man's wife is not reverencing and respecting him, he still has to love her as Christ loves the Church. Even if her husband is not loving her as Christ loves the Church, the wife still has to reverence and respect her husband.

Let's look again at **1 Peter 3:1**.

Likewise, ye wives, be in subjection to your own husbands; [Ladies, even if you are married to a man who is unsaved, that is no excuse to disrespect him, because God can save him through you.] *that, if any obey not the word* [talking about husbands], *they also may without the word be won by the conversation* [or lifestyle] *of the wives.*

This is an awesome principle. Notice it says, *that, if any obey not the word, they also may WITHOUT THE WORD* [In other words, the wife doesn't have to preach to her husband; she doesn't have to tell him she has to go to church all the time.], *be won by the conversation of the wives.*

1 Peter 3:2-4:

While they [the husbands] *behold your chaste conversation* [lifestyle] *coupled with fear.*

Whose adorning let it not be that outward adorning of plaiting the hair, and of wearing of gold, or of putting on of apparel [in other words, that is not the focus];

But let it be the hidden man of the heart, in that which is not corruptible, even the ornament of a meek and quiet spirit, which is in the sight of God of great price.

Many denominational churches teach that women are not to adorn themselves, but rather to look plain and unattractive. While the husbands go home and look at their unattractive wives, some are plotting to get next to the attractive women at work.

What God is doing here is making a comparison. He

is not saying not to fix up your hair, or wear gold and other jewelry, but He is saying put more emphasis on what Verse 4 says. This is what is important. But churches have used this scripture to tell women that they cannot wear any braids, gold, or other jewelry or fancy clothes.

I remember once my wife attended a certain church in my hometown, and the people looked at her as if she had a tail! She had on gold jewelry, a nice dress, and her hair was styled. I guess they thought she was a Jezebel, but this is not what God is talking about.

1 Peter 3:3-4

Whose adorning let it not be that outward adorning of plaiting the hair, and of wearing of gold, or of putting on of apparel;

But let it be the hidden man of the heart, in that which is not corruptible, even the ornament of a meek and quiet spirit, which is in the sight of God of great price.

I have heard some women say, *"I can't be meek and quiet. He'll run over me."* No, that is when he will stop running over you. Let me tell you a little secret. Your husband wants you because he saw the "soft and gentle" in you when you were courting. He didn't see Sapphire (a hard and boisterous woman); he saw "soft and gentle." He doesn't want a big mouth. He wants soft and gentle. He wants ladylike, frilly, nice, and feminine.

A woman can turn a man into a little puppy dog with "soft and gentle," but with a hard attitude, she will reap what she sows. You give him attitude, and you will get a pit bull. Attitude reaps attitude. *"My husband doesn't even tell me he loves me anymore."* I guess not, when you look at him like you do. Some wives need to change their attitudes. But they have to be taught; it is not something learned automatically.

68

Men have to be taught and women have to be taught; it is a two-way street.

The statement, *a meek and quiet spirit* should be underlined in every Christian woman's Bible. Notice what God says, *which is in the sight of God of great price.*

1 Peter 3:5-6

For after this manner in the old time the holy women also, who trusted in God, adorned themselves [with that meek and quiet spirit], *being in subjection unto their own husbands* [That is perhaps why some women do not reverence and respect their husbands, because they don't trust God]*:*

Even as Sara obeyed Abraham, calling him lord: whose daughters ye are, as long as ye do well, and are not afraid with any amazement.

Most women cannot even bring themselves to call their husbands lord. That is probably because of the way they have been trained. In the old days, women really respected their men. In fact, if these women did not show proper respect to their husbands, they would have been stoned. We are under grace now, so women act the way they want to act. Under the Law they acted the way they were supposed to, because if they didn't, it might have cost them their lives.

There are many unmarried women who desire husbands and who may not realize that they have "bad attitude" written invisibly across their foreheads. There are all kinds of attitudes: There is a sullen attitude, cocky attitude, "don't-need-no-man" attitude, and "you-can-go-you-know-where" attitude.

A lot of these attitudes come from women who have been hurt by men. These women have been misused and abused, so their attitudes are a sort of self-protection.

However, if a woman is not careful about her attitude, she can "protect" herself right out of a husband, because what a man is looking for is someone who is receptive, soft, and gentle. Men are basically all looking for the same thing; they are looking for someone to respond to them—not someone to talk back to them. They don't want attitude; they don't need attitude. They can get attitude all day long on the job, so why should they want to come home and get more of it?

Then the wife wonders why her husband doesn't want to come home. Well, if he has to look at her with her mouth poked out all the time, why should he want to come home? The questions women need to ask themselves if they can't seem to get their husbands to come home after work are: To what kind of attitude does he come home? Does he come home to a pleasant attitude? Does he get treated in such a way that he wants to come home?

You should be married to the one you consider your good friend. You should be able to laugh and joke and have fun with one another. People who have bad attitudes are no fun, and I don't care who they are. No one wants to be around anyone with a bad attitude, including people on your job. Bad attitudes turn people off.

Here is a quick, easy lesson on how to change your attitude: All you have to do is give people a nice big smile when you see them. You cannot smile and have an attitude at the same time—that is, if you are sincere. All husbands want when they come home is a good attitude with a nice smile and real loving concern. But guess what? You have to practice that. You know why? Because you have been "practicing" attitude too long. To change your bad attitude, you have to practice a good attitude, and one of the best ways of practicing a good attitude is to smile. It's the easiest thing in the world to do. Smiling makes you feel good; laughter makes you feel good. Everyone should have one movie video they keep around that makes them laugh and feel good —a movie that just turns your frown into a smile, then into pure laughter.

You might think you can just do it—*"I'm just going to start smiling."* No, change is not an automatic thing; change is something you have to work on and something you do because you want to do it. You purpose in your heart to change. A bad habit does not go away overnight. But if you keep working on it, change will take place. Then you can develop the habit of a good attitude.

So the number-one responsibility of the wife is to show reverence and respect to her husband. The wife should want to treat her husband like a king because he is coming home to his castle, and he is coming home to his queen. If he is not a king, then the wife is not a queen. If a man has a wife at home who treats him good, he wants to come home; he can't wait to get home, because his queen is there. He doesn't want to hear, *"Oh, it's you. You're home early."* He wants to hear, *"Oh, I'm so glad to have you home."*

If a wife does not show her husband reverence and respect, what makes you think the children will show him reverence and respect? If the husband doesn't show his wife reverence and respect, what makes him think the children will respect her?

Children mimic their parents. If the husband talks to his wife any kind of way, or the wife talks to the husband any kind of way, that is exactly what the children are going to do, because they see the parents doing these things to each other. Most lessons on how to treat people are learned at home. If the wife gives the husband a hard time, the children are watching and being taught.

If the wife says to her husband, *"Oh, you don't know what you are talking about,"* it should be no surprise when the children respond in like manner, *"Oh, Dad, you don't know what you are talking about."* They do this because they have heard their mother say the same thing.

You know this is true. How many times have you seen or heard a two- or three-year-old running around the house cursing when something happens he doesn't like? Where do you think the child learned that? Most of the time it came from the parents. I have seen it happen, and people thought it was cute. I didn't think it was cute. I thought it was sad, because it showed what was being said in that house. Children will say whatever they hear their parents say; they don't know they are not supposed to say those things. Then when the parents hear the child say something he is not supposed to say, they want to spank him for being bad. All the child is doing is saying what he has heard his parents say. The best way to have him not talk that way is for the parents not to talk that way.

The other reason you need to show reverence and respect to your mate at home is, you have to teach your children how to respect others. You have to teach your children at home because that is where respect is learned first.

NINE

RESPONSIBILITIES OF THE SPOUSES AND CHILDREN

In the previous chapter, we covered points on the responsibilities of the mother. I want to cover some other issues concerning the spouses and children in a blended-family setting.

Earlier, when I discussed the husband's responsibilities in the home, I emphasized that the father, according to the Bible, is considered the spiritual head of the family. He should be able to deal with both spiritual and natural principles. His primary responsibility, however, has more to do with making sure that the children understand the principles of loving God with all their hearts and with all their souls and with teaching them to fear (reverence) God. This is a vital principle that is not being taught enough today in Christian homes, and this lack of knowledge will negatively impact their lives later.

Titus 2:3-4 gives us more insight into things the mother is supposed to teach the children.

The aged women likewise, that they be in behav-

> *iour as becometh holiness, not false accusers, not given to much wine, teachers of good things;*
>
> *That they may teach the young women to be sober, to love their husbands, to love their children.*

God is giving a principle here that the women should be an example of holiness. In other words, God wants the young girls to see their mothers as holy women, not just as "old Mom." If they see them as holy women, children will have a better understanding of what a mother is supposed to be, and the girls will have someone to follow when it comes to raising their own children.

That they be in behaviour as becometh holiness.... In other words, the mother's holiness should be clearly seen. You can be holy and not show it, but God wants Christian women to show their daughters, or the young women with whom they come in contact, how to operate in holiness.

Verse 4 says that they may *teach* the young women. There are some things women need to be taught that are not automatically learned. The first thing it says is, women have to be taught to love their husbands. First, the woman has to understand what love is. Most people have a misconception of what love is. Too many people lock love into the physical relationship. Love is much more than physical. *Love* is a very broad word, and it has to do with your total commitment to a person. I like to give this definition, because it is the same definition that Jesus gives in **John 15:13**.

> *Greater love hath no man than this, that a man lay down his life for his friends.*

My definition for the highest kind of love is "dying to self for the purpose of being used by God to the fullest." So if love is dying to self, it means that you put the other person first. Imagine being in a relationship in which the wife puts the husband first, and the husband puts the wife first!

When my wife and I go out to eat, I always want to make sure we go where she wants to go. So, I'll say, *"Baby, where do you want to go?"* And she will reply, *"Baby, where do you want to go?"* We go back and forth with this because we are trying to put each other first.

One of my wife's favorite restaurants is a place I really don't like too well. One reason I don't particularly like this place is because of the strong garlic odor, but I will go to please my wife.

This is what I mean by putting another person's desire ahead of your own. Love is dying to self, and the Bible says the older women are to teach the younger women to put their husbands first. If they don't teach them, this is what can happen:

The wife will say, *"Well, he doesn't do this or that for me, and he doesn't say this or that to me."* In other words, she will begin to look at how her husband treats her. When we are looking at the other person's treatment of us, our focus really is on ourselves. *"He doesn't treat me this way; he doesn't treat me that way."* Love gives, and you reap what you sow **(Galatians 6:7)**. If you give what you say you want to receive, you will receive it back in return. But this principle has to be taught.

The reason women have to be taught to love their husbands is that as soon as they get married, some type of disagreement is bound to happen in the relationship. If a mother or someone more experienced has not prepared the woman for marriage, the unexpected situations that crop up in a marriage can throw her for a loop. You do not really know a person until you start living with that person, and people have some of the strangest, craziest habits.

A woman came in for counseling one time and told me that one of the things that bothered her about her husband was something she just could not figure out. He would come into the house and take off one shoe at the door so the carpet wouldn't get dirty. She appreciated the fact that he was willing to do take off his shoes as she asked, but he would keep walking through the house and take off the other shoe about 20 feet from where he left the first shoe. He would leave the shoes in two different places, and his wife would have to go and pick them up. This happened every day of the week.

She said to me, *"Pastor, it would be nice if he would drop the shoes in the same place. Why does he do this?"*

I said, *"Well, you married him, and that is what's in the cup."*

You may not know what is in the cup, but when you get married, you agree to drink everything that's in it! So do not get upset with a person just because he or she has some bad habits.

Teaching someone how to love is just simply teaching someone how to learn to put the other person first. Most people don't think about that, because they are usually going into the relationship because of a need they have. The Scriptures say the older women should teach the youngr ones to love. Love gives, and it does not look to receive all the time. People think that love is natural in a marriage and is just going to happen. No, it is not going to just happen; you have to share and communicate and make an effort to become a part of each other's lives.

When I first got married, I would blow in my wife's ear to be intimate with her, and I thought it turned her on. I did it once when we had been married about three years, and she yelled, *"Stop! I can't stand that."*

I didn't know she didn't like it because she never said anything before. You have to talk about these things; you have to talk about what a person likes or doesn't like. Just as knowing what pleases a wife sexually is not automatic, for a woman to love her husband is not automatic.

We have to always remember that marriage is two imperfect people coming together to form an imperfect relationship. When two people come together in marriage, they bring a lot of excess baggage (past challenges and bad habits). When the couple finally moves in together, he has his bags, and she has her bags, and when they start unpacking these bags, you can expect that there will be some chaos in the house.

The prospective spouses really need to get rid of a lot of those bags before marriage, but they often don't, and so they bring a lot of junk with them. For the relationship to be fulfilling, those bags have to be emptied and the stuff inside them thrown out. This means the spouses have to look in the mirror at themselves and work on their imperfections.

To work on your imperfections is the simplest thing in the world. All you have to do is to ask your spouse, *"What's wrong with me?"* Oh, he will communicate, all right! In fact, he (or she) will wear you out communicating what he (or she) believes is wrong with you. A lot of people don't really want to hear what their spouses have to say about them, and that is why they hesitate to ask such questions.

I had a counseling session in which the couple was just battling back and forth with one another. I said to the husband, *"Why don't you ask your wife what is wrong? I believe she will tell you the truth."* She was sitting there next to him and said, *"Yes, I'll tell you if you really want to know."* So he said, *"Go ahead and tell me in front of Pastor. Tell him how good I am to you."* He saw himself as some sort of Don Juan, the Lover. She said, *"You really want the truth? Well, you are lousy in bed."* She burst his bubble right there in front of me. He dropped his head and couldn't look up. He thought he was doing everything right, but he had never talked to her. He had never considered her feelings or what satisfied her. He was like most men. They never talk to their wives to find out what they need to know in order to please them. They are just like bulls in china closets, so to speak.

So if you want to find out about your imperfections, just ask your spouse. At the same time, also be willing to receive what your spouse has to say, and be willing to change.

When you give your spouse an opportunity to tell you what he or she thinks about you, it may not be what you want to hear. But if you will receive it and make an attempt to change, you can improve the relationship probably a hundredfold. No matter what it is or how bad it is, if you want to make a change, it can be done.

I recommend that the husband and wife take turns communicating their dislikes and what really bothers them. First the wife says what she doesn't like, then the husband. Go back and forth like that until all points have been brought up. Do it one point at a time. Talk about it, work on it. Figure out how to improve the situation.

You might think you are a great wife, but what does your husband think? You don't know because he has not told you what he thinks. The husband doesn't know what his wife thinks about him, because he has not asked her. It is amazing how spouses withhold information from one another. Yet in their hearts, they are thinking, *"I wish he would do this and do that."* Why don't you tell him? *"I wish she would do such and such."* Why don't you tell her?

If the spouses never tell each other what they want in the relationship, how can what they want come to pass? They have to be open and honest about what they expect and want from each other. Marriage is a lifetime commitment, or it should be, and who wants to go through life unfulfilled?

Many people have tried to learn on their own, sort of like on-the-job training, but most have not done a very good job with their marriage, and some are hanging on by their fingernails, because no one ever taught them how a marriage is really supposed to be.

I am constantly talking to my son about marriage. One day when we were driving down the street, I said, *"Son, don't try to figure them out. I would be a billionaire if I could figure out a woman. But your responsibility is to figure out yours. You have to get to know the woman that you marry; you have to get to understand her and that is a full-time job."*

I have not met one woman who is the same as another. And when I get to heaven, I am going to ask God why women will say one thing and mean another. I am not talking about anything specifically, but women have this knack for saying one thing and meaning something totally different, and it can drive men up a wall.

I know some women who will not be forthright with their husbands for anything. It may be that they don't want to hurt their feelings. Let's say the husband goes shopping and buys a suit and tie. He's so proud of himself, and he comes out dressed in his new outfit and says to his wife, *"How do you like it?"*

She says, *"Oh, it looks nice."* She should tell him what she really thinks. She should say, *"Honey, that plaid tie doesn't look good with that striped suit."*

Husbands and wives lie to each other all the time. A wife prepares her husband a new dish for dinner. She asks her husband, *"How do you like it?"* He tells her, *"Oh, it's good."* He just lied, because what he was really thinking was, *"I hope she never fixes this dish again."* But she will, because he said it was good. So he will see it again, especially if it is easy for her to make.

I tell the truth. If my wife prepares something I don't like, I tell her, *"Please don't ever fix that for me again."* Because you didn't tell your wife how you really felt, you may have

79

to eat that same dish again and again. It serves you right, because you should have been honest the first time.

Telling the truth is a way of improving the marriage relationship. Of course, there is always the proper way to say something. You don't say, *"I don't like this mess,"* about her cooking after she has slaved six hours over it. Speak the truth in love. Say something, such as, *"Baby, this really is not one of my favorite types of meal, but I appreciate your wanting to give me a new dish."*

God made the ultimate sacrifice when he offered up His only Son on the cross for the benefit of all mankind. That is love. Are you willing to sacrifice yourself for your mate? If you love him or her that much, you will not be in divorce court. People head for divorce court because over a period of time, there are so many things they don't like about their mates, and they reach a point where they say, *"I am tired of this. I want out."*

They have based their relationship on things they don't like. When they said, *"I do,"* all the things they liked and didn't like were already there. The bags came in with both of them. Since the two of them did not work on the problems, they were magnified over a period of time.

Love does not walk out the door when things are not going so great. Love looks for a way to improve a situation. Love looks at a way to get God involved. Love teaches a woman how to pray for her husband, how to intercede to turn a situation around, how to cast her care on the Lord and not turn her back on her man.

A mother has to teach her daughter and prepare her for marriage, but she cannot teach her daughter if she does not know herself. People have a tendency to teach their children based on what they have gone through, and how they handled a situation, although they have not necessarily handled it correctly. *"This is what happened to me. This is how*

I handled that situation. Don't let him do this to you."

A mother who says these things is poisoning her daughter's mind. Who says her daughter will marry a man who is going to do the same thing to her? We have to teach our children biblical principles that will help them deal with the issues of daily living. It is the parents' responsibility to teach their children how to love their spouses and how to communcate properly and function successfully in a marriage relationship. One aspect of good communication between spouses is the willingness and the ability to encourage one another.

Deuteronomy 3:28

But charge Joshua, and encourage him, and strengthen him....

Husbands need to encourage their wives. When she cooks a meal he really likes, he needs to tell her, *"Baby, that was a good meal."* When the husband cuts the grass and makes the yard look nice, the wife should tell him, *"Honey, you made the yard really look nice today."* When he's out there washing the cars and spends half the day shining them up, she should get in her car and say, *"Oh, baby, you did such a beautiful job; the car looks new."* Everybody likes words of encouragement.

Responsibilities of the Children

It is very important that the children understand biblical principles also. **Ephesians 6:1-3** states:

Children, obey your parents in the Lord: for this is right.

Honour thy father and mother; (which is the first commandment with promise;)

81

***That it may be well with thee, and thou mayest
live long on the earth.***

I like to stress Verse 3, especially when I am teaching
children to obey their parents. In other words, if the children
obey and honor their parents, things will go right for them.
Consequently, if they disrespect, dishonor, and disobey their
parents, life is going to be hard for them, plus they will die
early. This is what God says in His Word, and I believe it.

In fact, the suicide rate among young people is going
off the map; young people are committing suicide in
alarmingly rising numbers, saying, *"I am unhappy at home
and you're unhappy at home; let's go somewhere and kill ourselves."*
This is becoming a common occurrence among teenagers,
and it doesn't matter what the race. It is happening all the
time. Why? No one has ever taught these children biblical
principles to live by, or the fact that they have to honor their
fathers and their mothers.

Children who are a part of a blended family have to be
taught to obey the new parent. If it is the mother with the
children, she has to tell her children before she gets married,
*"I am getting ready to get married; this will be my husband, and he
will be your stepfather, and you will have to obey him."* Children
have to be taught this. Young people, especially teenagers,
will say something like, *"You're not my daddy; you can't tell me
anything."*

This is evidence that the mother did not instill
obedience in that child, because his or her responsibility
is to obey that man. If the man is going to take on the
responsibility of providing housing for the children, feeding
them, and generally taking care of the family, the children
will have to obey him. They may not like it, but they will still
have to do it. We all have to do things we do not like to do;
that is what life is about. That is part of training the children

for life, and it is good training to make children do some things they don't want to do.

Actually, success in life is based on how well we handle the difficulties of living, and children need to be taught this fact. When you know how to handle the difficulties, you can enjoy a good life.

Children must understand what the Bible means when it says, ***that it may be well with thee.*** God says if we obey His Word, things will be well with us. Children have to be taught that they have to obey their parents and stepparents primarily because *God* says to obey, not because the *parents* say to obey. The parent has to tell the child, *"God says that if you obey, honor* [which means 'highly respect'] *us as your parents, it will be well with you; things will work out for you. You will live long on the earth."*

A lot of gang members do not expect to live past age 25. Why? Because they have disrespected so many people, including their parents. That is the penalty for disrespect.

If you don't respect the law, you will probably wind up in prison or in an early grave. People are in prison because they did not respect the law. People are on death row because they did not respect the law. Respect is not something that is acquired; it has to be taught. Parents are not teaching their children how to show respect to authority. That is why the children are having a tough time.

Proverbs 22:6 says, ***Train up a child in the way he should go....*** People really should not have children until they are ready to be parents. The wife says, *"I want a baby."* The husband says, *"Okay."* So they make a baby, and the baby comes, but in many cases, they are nowhere near ready for that baby; they know nothing about what it takes to raise children biblically, physically, or financially.

When children come into the world, they make noise, they cry, they want attention and care, and sometimes young parents are not ready for that. All things being equal, babies are easy to take care of; they will not normally cry if they are dry and full, unless they are sick or awakened with a nightmare or some other similar situation.

This is how babies train the parents: After the babies are put into their cribs, they cry, and the parents go and pick them up. The parents don't take time to see if it is feeding time or if the baby's diaper is wet. If the baby is full and the diaper is dry, instead of comforting the baby through touch and letting him or her go back to sleep, they pick up the baby every time he or she cries. The baby concludes, if you will, through the established pattern, *"Umm, I cry and they pick me up."* So the baby begins to train the parents.

There really is no such thing as bad children—just "bad" or misinformed parents who don't know how to get their children to do what they are supposed to do. Wayward teenagers often get a bad rap, when really it is the parents who are to blame. Show your children a lot of love and affection, and you will be surprised at what they will do for you. Basically, all they are looking for is some attention, and when they get it—and, of course, love goes with the attention—they will do what you tell them to do. Children are all different; what ministers love to one might not be what ministers love to another. And parents have to realize this and discover how to show love to each of their children.

The first responsibility of the child is to learn to be obedient to the parents and to others in authority.

Romans 12:1-2

I beseech you therefore, brethren, by the mercies of God, that ye present your bodies a living sacrifice, holy, acceptable unto God, which is your reasonable service.

And be not conformed to this world: but be ye transformed by the renewing of your mind, that ye may prove what is that good, and acceptable, and perfect, will of God.

Children, too, must learn to submit their will to God's will. Children always come up with, *"I want."* You have to teach your child to submit to God at a young age. This will help them later on in life. The reason children don't know how to submit to authority is, they have not been trained to submit to their parents. Further, no one has ever taught them the importance of submitting to God. When we "train up a child," there are biblical principles that we have to give them. We have to teach them to love God with all their hearts, souls, and minds. We have to teach them to have a reverence and a respect for God, but we also have to teach them how to submit to God's will.

When the parents teach the children this, the parents have to help the children understand that sometimes things are not going to go their way. Sometimes other people will have control over them, and they will have to submit to their will. If children understood this, it would be easier for them to submit to teachers who have the responsibility of helping to educate them. But when they get to school, they don't want to do what the teachers tell them because the parents have not taught them to submit at home.

Another thing a child must do is to understand the importance of learning.

2 Timothy 2:15

Study to shew thyself approved unto God, a workman that needeth not to be ashamed, rightly dividing the word of truth.

The reason children come home and say, *"I don't*

like school," is because the parents have never spent time stressing the importance of learning and gaining knowledge. The parents have to show the children the importance of education so they can be successful in life. Learning is the key, and learning is a process of line upon line, precept upon precept, and it all happens over a period of time—a *long* period of time. Parents must learn to motivate their children as a part of the process.

TEN

Understanding the Dynamics of Marriage Within the Blended Family

In this concluding chapter, I want to summarize some of the things I have covered in previous chapters, as well as cover other essential issues that need to be in place if the blended family is to be a successful family unit.

A blended family is two people coming together with children from previous relationships, and because the spouses have these children from previous relationships, there may be relatives involved who are not a part of the immediate family, but who have been a part of the children's lives prior to the parent's remarriage. These relationships cannot be discarded or discounted; they are a part of the blended family.

If the primary relationship—that is, the man and woman—is not handled with wisdom and understanding, based on the Word of God, the new marriage and its challenges can be absolute nightmares. If the children in the blended family are not made to understand the new relationship, it will be particularly traumatic for them, and, consequently, for the parents as well. If the spouses do not know how to handle the challenges that arise in a blended family, the devil can drive a wedge between the couple and hurt, or even destroy, the relationship.

One of the things that happens, and I want to say this particularly to the women (but also to the men, because men have been guilty of this too), when you get married, you have to make sure that those children become *our* children and not just *my* children. If you consider them as only *your* children, you will take offense to something your spouse may say to the children, which can cause a problem. When a couple gets married, they really have to make an effort to have a special relationship with one another, because the children can come between them if those children sense any weakness in the couple's relationship.

Proverbs 4:1-5

Hear, ye children, the instruction of a father, and attend to know understanding.

For I give you good doctrine, forsake ye not my law.

For I was my father's son, tender and only beloved in the sight of my mother.

He taught me also, and said unto me, Let thine heart retain my words: keep my commandments, and live.

Get wisdom, get understanding: forget it not....

Wisdom is the ability to apply knowledge. Understanding is simply the process it takes to apply that knowledge. You can have knowledge of a principle, but what about understanding how the principle works? For example, many ministers often tell their congregations to pray, but if I were to ask how many people could name at least five of the different types of biblical prayer, not many would be able to do so.

I can say, *"Pray,"* but if you don't understand all the ways of praying according to the Bible, and if you don't have a clear understanding of how to pray, even though you may be praying the best way you know how, it is not necessarily going to be the right way to pray. Knowledge of prayer is one thing, but understanding how to pray correctly is something totally different. Not only do you have to get the wisdom (ability to apply knowledge) but you also have to have a clear understanding of what you are doing, or you will not be able to do it right.

People understand the term, *"getting married."* Nevertheless most people do not realize what marriage is all about until they actually get into it. According to this proverb, you can get an understanding of marriage prior to getting into a marriage.

Solomon said, *"Get wisdom, but get understanding also."* In a blended-family situation, you need to get an understanding of what you are getting into before you go into the marital relationship, because, if the relationship is not of God, the dynamics of marriage within the blended family can wreak havoc in the lives of everyone involved, especially the children. Look at **Proverbs 4:5-7.**

> **Get wisdom, get understanding: forget it not; neither decline from the words of my mouth.**
>
> **Forsake her not, and she shall preserve thee: love**

her, and she shall keep thee.

Wisdom is the principal thing; therefore get wisdom: and with all thy getting get understanding.

Those already in a blended-family situation and those planning to enter into one need to get wisdom and understanding of how to apply the principles that will help them have successful family relationships so they can enjoy the fruits of a blessed marriage.

Dynamics Involved in the Blended-Family Relationship

Marriage is marriage and family is family. However, the blended family has a uniqueness of its own. The following are some suggestions for helping the family move toward being a complete unit.

1. **The new stepparent MUST show the new mate love and affection that the children can see.**

   In my family, as I was growing up, a man and a woman did not publicly show any type of affection toward one another. I never saw my mother and stepfather kiss or hug one another. In fact, I never saw anyone in my family kiss or hug one another. In many cultures in times past, expressions of affection, even among family members, was considered taboo. You never saw anyone be affectionate.

   Children need to see their parents interacting with one another in an affectionate way. If the only thing they ever see between the couple is conversation, they may not know how to relate affectionately to their mates when they get married.

   In a new relationship, it is important that the children

90

see that the new spouse loves those kids' mom or dad. The only way they can see this is if they see some visible signs of affection, such as the mates putting their arms around each other, kissing when they come home, or kissing when they leave the house. There doesn't have to be anything way out; simply some basic show of affection can work wonders for the kids.

Children will think, *"They must really care about each other. Every time he comes home, they kiss and hug, and every time he leaves, he says goodbye with a kiss or a hug."* This adds a degree of stability to the home life of the children, as well as makes the children more comfortable with the relationship.

If the children never see this affection between the new mates, and they saw it with the ex-mate, they may begin to wonder, *"Well, why did Mom marry him, and she was always kissing on Dad?"* The kids are going to be a little confused. It is extremely important for the children to see some expressions of love between the parent and stepparent. Children are quick to think, *"Something is wrong. Evidently, she doesn't like him, so I'm going to stick close to Mom."*

2. The stepparent MUST show the children love.

Children develop insecurities very quickly. It is important that the children feel comfortable in the relationship from the start. Part of showing children you care about them is learning how to show affection so that the children are comfortable with it. What do I mean? Let's say you get married, and your spouse has a 12-year-old son. A 12-year-old boy may not want the parent or stepparent to hug him; he may not be into hugging, maybe because no one ever hugged him before. My son is in his 20s, and we still hug, but then I brought him up that way. But for a lot of teenaged boys, both younger and older, hugging is not something they are used to doing because *macho* men don't hug. The stepparent has to find out what is comfortable for that child, and he has to make an overt effort to let the child know that he cares about him and wants to do whatever is going to work as a way of showing affection to the child, whether shaking hands, "high-fiving," or whatever.

If a girl is involved, females like conversation and compliments, "*Oh, that is a pretty dress you have on today; you sure look pretty in that color.*" In other words, the stepparent makes a real effort to show an interest in the child, and when he does this, the child will think that the stepparent really does care about her.

What happens too often when people get married is, they only think about one another. They act like they are two peas in a pod, but what about those other little peas involved? If you want to do this right, you have to really be concerned about the children. Yes, for the couple, it will be easy to show one another love, but it is going to require some extra effort on the part of the stepparent to show the children love and affection. Of course, it will not all be in the same manner, because all children are different.

All children may not be receptive to the type of affection you may be showing them. You may have to do one thing for one child and something totally different for another child. Then you have to be careful in situations where there is more than one child. You can't show favoritism. The parent is in big trouble if he shows favoritism. The stepparent has to make sure to treat all the children equally.

Raising children is work. It requires you to think and even to write some things down so you don't forget them. Just remember, you chose to go into the relationship. You chose to marry someone with kids, so you have to learn how to co-exist happily in the relationship, and it may take considerable effort on your part to pull it off. If you don't put forth the effort, or you only love the parent and not the children, you are entering a situation in which you cannot even begin to imagine the problems you are creating for yourself, as well as for the children. You are molding these children's lives from the first day, and you are molding them for life. If you do not like the kids, they will know it. They will probably dislike you, too, and then in their minds, they will think, for example, *"Mom got married, but she married a guy who doesn't like us."* So these children will develop insecurities before you are settled in the house.

Children want to be loved just like everybody else; in fact, they probably need love more than adults do. If the prospective mate does not like the children, he or she should not marry into this blended-family situation, because there is nothing but trouble ahead for the whole family.

When a couple gets married, they are all wrapped up in each other and they often forget about the kids. The couple cannot do that. That new spouse absolutely *must* show the children love, and it has to be a visible thing, not something the stepparent just talks about.

3.   The parent with the children has to show that he or she loves the new spouse.

The children have to see that the parent loves the new spouse, and they have to see it in a special way. If the children know that the parent loves the new spouse and that they cannot drive a wedge between the two, it will help the kids act a lot better. If there are any signs of wavering on the part of the parent with regard to showing love for the new spouse, the children will take advantage of the situation and cause problems for the stepparent.

If the parent says something about the stepparent indirectly, such as, *"I know it is not the way we used to do it, but you know this is just the way he [or she] is."* Or the parent could say the wrong thing directly to the kids about the new spouse that can create a problem for the new spouse, because the children will begin to openly disrespect him or her.

So the parent has to show the new spouse love and respect, and the kids have to see it. They need to be able to say with conviction, *"Mom [or Dad] really loves her [or his] new husband [or wife]."* And they have to know this in their hearts, because it will affect how they act.

4. During the process of adjustment, the natural parent can in no way forsake the children.

This happens in many new relationships, particularly if the parent has been unmarried for a period of time. He is so glad to find her that he spends a lot of time with the person even to the detriment of the children. The first thing that happens following the marriage ceremony—and most children don't understand this—is that the couple goes off on a honeymoon for a week or two, leaving the children to stay with relatives or whomever. No one sat down and explained to the children what a honeymoon is all about. So the children are often left with someone they do not necessarily want to be with, and their lives and living arrangements are disrupted, even if only for two weeks.

When the couple comes back, they spend all their time talking about their honeymoon, and they forget that they left the children in an environment that was not really comfortable for them. Then the kids say, for example, *"She loves him more than she loves us."* Sometimes they even verbalize this to the parent. But more than verbalize it, they will begin to act out their resentment. Moreover, this resentment will manifest in their schoolwork and in their relationships with others. Whereas, before, they were getting good grades, now, suddenly, they are getting bad grades. Before, they were not having a behavioral problem in school. Now, suddenly, they are talking and acting up. They are trying to get attention at school because they are not getting it at home. It is not that they want the attention from the new spouse, but the real parent is showing so much love and attention to him or her that the children feel left out.

This usually happens when a man or a woman is just so glad to be with an adult and finally have someone to talk to about adult things. They have been talking to the kids for five years. When you talk to kids every day for five years, you are glad to talk to an adult. Still, there has to be a balance, and the children have to understand what is going on. Things have to be done gradually, and the best way to do them is to bring the children along slowly and explain to them what is happening each step of the way. The parent has to constantly show that he still loves and cares about the children.

The children can get along without ever loving the new spouse, but they cannot get along without loving the natural parent. Any neglect of the children by the parent will affect them in a tremendously negative way. The parent has to be able to establish and maintain a loving relationship with the children, even though a new spouse is on the scene. It is a very delicate balance, because the children have to know that the parent loves the new spouse, but they still have to know that parent loves them too; it is something that both spouses have to work on.

I grew up in a blended-family relationship, but I didn't like the one I grew up in. I would not wish it on my worst enemy. The way I grew up was no fun to me. My stepfather didn't care about me or my brothers and sister. He treated my mom like a queen, but he didn't care anything about the children. I had to live five years in that environment, and I couldn't wait to get away. My mother was happy because she was married to a man who was taking good care of her. No one seemed to care how the kids felt, except my grandmother and my aunt, but nobody in the home seemed to care about what we thought or how we felt. So I know what I am talking about. I lived it, and I have to counsel people on a daily basis who are going through, or have been through, these types of situations. You cannot forget about your children. Praise God that He brought a good man or a good woman into your life, but you cannot forget about the children you already have.

5.   To avoid these challenges, the parents MUST understand the importance of constant communication with everyone involved.

The husband and wife must talk to each other; the husband must talk to the children; the wife must talk to the children; and the husband and the wife must talk to the children together. There is a constant communication flow that has to take place in the blended-family relationship, and it never stops until the children are grown and on their own.

Parents have to be so concerned about the children that they will be aware of any mood changes. If you are communicating with your children on a consistent basis, you will notice a mood change in a child, and that is usually a sign that something is wrong. Suddenly, a child who is normally a happy child comes home, goes into his room, closes the door, and doesn't want to talk. Something is wrong. You ask, *"What's wrong?"* *"Nothing,"* he says. Don't accept that. Make him talk. Pull it out of him. Don't accept *"nothing,"* because he has just lied to you. If it were nothing, he would not be acting the way he is acting. With children, sometimes you have to pull it out of them. You have to sit there and let them know that you care about how they are feeling and that you care about the things that affect them. You care because they appear to be unhappy, and you do not want to see them unhappy. The bottom line is that the parent *must* keep the lines of communication open between the parent and child at all times.

Communication is the key to avoiding major problems in a blended family. When people are talking, they can begin to at least see what is going on. Problems usually exist in families where there is no communication, even between husband and wife. If a couple is having problems, it is because they are not communicating with one another.

The number-one area where husbands and wives do not communicate is sex. People assume that everybody knows what to do. It's the biggest mistake you can ever make. People are different, and when you get married, that person does not know you, and you do not really know him or her. To find out what each likes requires communication.

People would be shocked at the number of men and women who refuse to talk about these issues. I have to deal with these issues all the time in counseling sessions; people are having challenges because they never talk to each other about the things causing them problems.

The second area that people do not want to communicate about is the marriage itself—things that bother them in the marriage. People have their own way of thinking, and they assume that the person they are involved with thinks the way they do. I said it before, but it bears repeating: Marriage is simply two imperfect people coming together to form an imperfect relationship. If people talked more about working things out in the marriage, they might not be so quick to go to divorce court.

6. **The parent of the children MUST be in one accord with the new spouse concerning discipline.**

People have different ideas of discipline. Let's say a man marries a woman with three children, and the man and woman don't talk about disciplining the children. The husband grew up in a family where his parents taught him biblical principles, and they believed in spanking children. He got spanked, his sisters got spanked, his brothers got spanked, so he believes in spanking the children. So if they act up, he's looking for a paddle!

(The way I grew up, you didn't get spanked with your clothes on. Our parents would pull down our pants to spank us. I, my sister, and my brothers were brought up this way.)

The wife in this hypothetical situation grew up a little bit differently. She has raised her children all by herself for the last five years, and she has an understanding with these children, and she does not believe in spanking her kids. She believes in deprivation punishment of some sort. She will give them a time out and have them go sit in a corner, or she'll restrict their television time or take away the privilege altogether for a while.

The couple gets married, but they did not talk about discipline. In about two weeks, the nine-year-old son decides to pitch a fit; he is going to be disobedient. Well, the new dad decides the boy needs a spanking and starts to pull off his belt, but the wife wants to call the cops. *"You are not going to whip my child!"* (See, now it is *her* child.)

Confusion and anger come between the spouses and the children, all because the husband and wife never talked before the marriage about how they were going to discipline the children. This may be an extreme case, but it happens. Or maybe the husband says to the child, *"You go to your room, and you just stay there."* No matter what he does, since they haven't discussed discipline, the mother is going to be upset. This is usually the first point that begins to drive people apart in a relationship like this. When one of the parties decides to discipline the other's child, the fight is on!

The couple has to be in one accord when it comes to disciplining the children. There are two good reasons why. First of all, the spouses have to keep peace between the two of them, so that the enemy cannot drive a wedge between them. Second, the children need to know that the spouses are in one accord. They need to know that more than anything else. Even with their natural parents in a natural-parent environment, kids need to understand that they cannot get anything over on Mom, because Dad is going to back her up. And they cannot get anything over on Dad, because Mom is going to back him up. Kids are smart. As they get older, kids get real slick at "playing" the parents, and they do it in such a way that they will have the husband and wife battling each other while they are sitting in the corner giggling. So the parents have to be in one accord as it relates to disciplining the children, and they had better talk about this before they get married. If not, the devil will have the children acting up as soon as they are all in the house together.

7.   **The mates MUST understand the importance of constant activity and interaction as a family.**

Even natural families don't do this enough. Everyone goes his separate way. For the family to be strong, the parents have to pull the family together. Although I did not like a lot of things about my stepfather, one of the things he did for us was to take us out to eat together as a family at least once a week. Back then, there were what we called drive-in restaurants. People would sit in their cars, and the waitress would take your order and bring the food to your car. We would go to a restaurant like that or to a sit-down restaurant every Thursday evening, and we could order whatever we wanted off the menu. (We were not limited in what we ordered, but the drawback was that you had to eat all that you ordered. That made us careful of what we ordered, because if we didn't eat all of the food we ordered, the next week, we would not get anything to eat, and we would have to sit in the car while everyone else ate.)

We looked forward to every Thursday. We would be so excited that during the day, we would be talking about what we were going to order that night. There were five of us—three kids and my mother and stepfather. The adults would sit in the front seat, and the three kids in the back. I remember those Thursday "eat-outs" as being the most fun thing we ever did as a family. One day a week, we interacted with one another. To me, that was the best day of the week. We went to church together, but there was no interaction. But on Thursday night, there would be interaction. My mother would be talking to us; my stepfather would be talking to us, and the children would be talking and laughing with one another. There was family interaction. I believe this interaction is what is missing in a lot of families today.

In a blended-family situation, family interaction is paramount if the parents want to establish a comfortable family relationship with the children. It doesn't matter where you go, whether it's out to eat pizza together or to the movies, as long as the family does it together. Teenagers will fight the parents on this, but teens need to be a part of this interaction too. They need to know that as long as they are living in the home, they are a part of the family times of interacting as a family, and they need to be told by the parent, *"Hey, I don't care if you are nineteen, we are still going out to eat together as a family, and you are going out with your five-year-old brother."*

Teens get too old for their little brothers and sisters, but you have to teach them that this is something the family is going to do together. These outings would help any family, not just the blended family.

8.   The parent with the children MUST put the new

spouse first in the eyes of the children.

This may seem to be a contradiction, but it is not. The children need to know the spiritual priorities are: God, Jesus the Son, the Holy Spirit, man, woman, child. That is biblical order. What has happened in many families is that the mother will put the children above the new spouse. Children should never ever see that; they must know that the new spouse is important. They have to know this, because if not, especially with teenagers, they will figure out a way to drive the couple apart; they will figure out a way to make their lives a living hell. This has to go both ways. You can never put your children above your mate, and your children have to understand that. Once they understand that, they will fall right in line and not try to drive a wedge between the spouses.

(1)   **The new spouse MUST not be jealous of the natural parent's relationship with the children.**

(2)   **The children MUST be taught not to be jealous of the new spouse or to feel left out. The parent has to teach the children this. They are a very important part of the relationship. This needs to be constantly reinforced by both parents.**

(3)   **The parent with the children MUST help the new spouse to understand that the children are *our* children, and not just *my* children. Thus the new spouse MUST assume the full responsibility of being a parent.**

Every aspect of our Christian life has to be based on the Word of God. The Bible plainly tells us that *we walk by faith and not by sight* (**2 Corinthians 5:7**). In other words, we need to learn to live our lives based on biblical principles; we need to learn to pray together; we need to learn to purpose in our hearts to set these four goals in our families. If we do, we will never have a problem.

(1)   To love one another.

(2)   To consider one another.

(3)   To understand one another.

(4)   To be in one accord with one another so that the enemy cannot get in.

1 John 5:4

For whatsoever is born of God overcometh the world: and this is the victory that overcometh the world, even our faith.

As we apply biblical principles to our lives, as we teach our children to live by these biblical principles, as we live our lives based on biblical principles, there is no way the enemy can drive a wedge between the members in the family, whether it is a blended family or a natural family. However, if we try to live our lives based on what we think, or on past experiences, we are destined to fail in our quest for total family unity, peace, and joy. We must learn how to live by God's Word if we are to be successful in this life.

ABOUT THE AUTHOR

Dr. Alfred D. Harvey, Jr. founded St. Louis Christian Center on January 7, 1994. He received the vision for the church on August 14, 1983, while flying to New York from Los Angeles to assist with Dr. Frederick K.C. Price's Ever Increasing Faith Ministries crusade. While high over the city of St. Louis, Dr. Harvey heard God speak these words to his spirit: "You will have a large church in St. Louis." Even though his wife, Loretta, was born and raised in St. Louis, it had never occurred to either of them to leave Los Angeles for St. Louis. Dr. Harvey was surprised to hear that promise from the Lord. They arrived in the St. Louis area in December 1993 and have never looked back.

True to the promise, since its beginning, SLCC has grown steadily in both location and membership, and currently has well over 5,000 persons on its membership rolls and a staff of more than 30 full-time ministry workers. In 1998, SLCC purchased a 30-plus-acre parcel with a 28,000-square-foot building containing a 1,500-seat sanctuary, administrative offices, and conference area. A secondary 10,000-square-foot building houses its children's services and special activities. The church is fast outgrowing these facilities and larger facilities are in the making.

The church has five services a week, including two Sunday morning services, midweek intercessory prayer, and midweek day and evening Bible studies. SLCC also has a radio outreach program, Doers of the Word Ministries, which airs three times a day Monday through Friday, in which Dr. Harvey ministers on the subjects of faith, the Holy Spirit, prayer, marriage, and raising children.

Born and raised in Los Angeles, California, Dr. Harvey

received his spiritual training from Dr. Price, founder and pastor of Crenshaw Christian Center. As a member of CCC for more than 16 years, Dr. Harvey served faithfully in the following positions: executive board, counselor and counselor trainer, choir member, assistant youth director, youth worker and teacher, usher, vice president for special affairs with the CCC Men's Fellowship, advisor to the street witnessing team, advisor to the intercessory prayer group, dean of student affairs with the CCC Ministry Training Institute, and instructor in the CCC School of Ministry.

A retired police officer with more than 25 years of service, Dr. Harvey left the Los Angeles Police Department in 1989 to enter full-time ministry. His call was to teach those entering the ministry, as well as those who have a desire to have a more intensive knowledge of God's Word. He served in this capacity until God summoned him to follow the promise and establish a "Word" church in St. Louis, teaching and preaching the full counsel of God according to the Holy Bible.

Dr. and Mrs. Harvey, who are the parents of three children and three grandchildren, reside in a St. Louis suburb.

OTHER GREAT BOOKS BY DR. HARVEY

Study to shew thyself approved unto God,
a workman that needeth not to be ashamed,
rightly dividing the word of truth.
(2 Timothy 2:15)

How to Develop Your Heavenly Prayer Language — In all spiritual things, we must grow up and develop. It is imperative that you develop an articulate prayer language and are effective as you pray in the Spirit. Satan often uses spiritual warfare to hinder you from learning how to develop and use your prayer language. This dynamic teaching will help you remove the fear and emotional aspects that hinder many from using their heavenly prayer language. The rumors that have spread through many churches and have perverted the use of speaking in tongues in the minds of many Christians are dispelled. See through Scripture how to develop proper control and effectively use your own heavenly prayer language.

Thank You, Jesus, for My Healing! — Dr. Harvey writes, "You have to understand where sickness and disease come from if you're going to combat them successfully. If Jesus went about doing good and healing all who were oppressed of the devil [Acts 10:38], then why is it that so many people believe God puts sickness on them?" Dr. Harvey makes his point very plain: "God is not glorified through your sickness, nor is He trying to make you humble. The devil is trying to kill you!"

The Law of Respect: A Wisdom Principle for Teens and Adults
Dr. Harvey shares a profound message for teenagers and adults. Although it is increasingly de-emphasized in our modern world, God felt this principle was important enough to include it in the Ten Commandments; it's called respect and it's a law. Whether your parents are living or dead, you dare not neglect this teaching!

AUDIO RECORDINGS OF TEACHING BY DR. HARVEY

So then faith cometh by hearing,
and hearing by the word of God.
Romans 10:17

Don't Miss the Benediction ($20)

GO!—A Command to Every Believer ($40)

Intercessory Prayer ($5)

Principles of Prayer Parts1 through 8
(call for pricing)

Qualifications for Successful Ministry Part 1 ($50)

Qualifications for Successful Ministry Part 2 ($50)

Qualifications for Successful Ministry Part 3 ($50)

Seven Keys to a Happy Marriage (Male Perspective) ($40)

Silent Prayer: Truth or Lie? ($10)

Six Principles to Get Rid of Lust Forever ($30)

The Limitless Power of Unity ($20)

The Lord's Prayer Is Not for Christians ($5)

Tithes & Offerings: Keys to Unlocking God's
Revelation Knowledge ($50)

Giving and Receiving ($30)

Please specify cassette or CD format

To place an order, call
1-866-319-7460
or send in the order form provided.

Quick Order Form

Fax orders: Fax this completed form to (314) 867-2873.

Telephone orders: Call (866) 319-7460 toll free.

Email orders: Transmit the information below to orders@slcc.org.

Postal orders: Send this form to Doers Publishing,
P.O. Box 38700, St. Louis, MO 63138.

Please send the following books and/or audio recordings. I understand that I may return defective items for exchange within 30 days of receipt.

Quantity	Title	Total
___	_____	$ _____
___	_____	$ _____
___	_____	$ _____
___	_____	$ _____
___	_____	$ _____
___	_____	$ _____
___	_____	$ _____

Name: _____

Address: _____

City/State/Zip: _____

Telephone (with area code): _____

Email address: _____

Shipping (add to the total cost of the order):
U.S.: $2 for first book or audio recording; $1 for each additional item
Outside U.S.: Call for rates (866) 319-7460.

Payment Method (check one):

__ Check (made payable to SLCC)

__ Credit Card (check one; provide number, name, expiration date, & signature):

__ Visa   __ MasterCard   __ American Express

Card number: _____

Name as it appears on the card: _____

Expiration date (MM/YYYY): _____

Signature: _____

Quick Order Form

Fax orders: Fax this completed form to (314) 867-2873.
Telephone orders: Call (866) 319-7460 toll free.
Email orders: Transmit the information below to orders@slcc.org.
Postal orders: Send this form to Doers Publishing,
  P.O. Box 38700, St. Louis, MO 63138.

Please send the following books and/or audio recordings. I understand that I may return defective items for exchange within 30 days of receipt.

Quantity	Title	Total
——	_____	$ _____
——	_____	$ _____
——	_____	$ _____
——	_____	$ _____
——	_____	$ _____
——	_____	$ _____
——	_____	$ _____

Name: _____

Address: _____

City/State/Zip: _____

Telephone (with area code): _____

Email address: _____

Shipping (add to the total cost of the order):
U.S.: $2 for first book or audio recording; $1 for each additional item
Outside U.S.: Call for rates (866) 319-7460.

Payment Method (check one):
__ Check (made payable to SLCC)
__ Credit Card (check one; provide number, name, expiration date, & signature):

__ Visa   __ MasterCard   __ American Express

Card number: _____

Name as it appears on the card: _____

Expiration date (MM/YYYY): _____

Signature: _____